Geography 21

EUROPE

EUROPE

Simon Ross
Head of Geography, Queen's College Taunton

Series Consultant: Michael Raw
Head of Geography, Bradford Grammar School

Collins
Educational
An Imprint of HarperCollins*Publishers*

CONTENTS

CHAPTER 1 A sense of place   4
Unit 1: What is Europe?

CHAPTER 2 Weather and climate   12
Unit 1: The weather in Europe
Unit 2: The climate of Europe
Unit 3: Enquiry: Mediterranean and sub-Arctic climates

CHAPTER 3 Rivers   20
Unit 1: River study: The Coquet, Northumberland, UK
Unit 2: Managing the River Rhine
Unit 3: Flooding!

CHAPTER 4 Farming   38
Unit 1: The farm system
Unit 2: Farming case study: Aviaries Farm, UK
Unit 3: Types of farming in Europe
Unit 4: Leisure Farms: farms of the future?
Unit 5: The Common Agricultural Policy

CHAPTER 5 Energy   56
Unit 1: Types of energy
Unit 2: Non-renewable energy: oil
Unit 3: Renewable energy: wind
Unit 4: Conserving energy

CHAPTER 6 Ice   68
Unit 1: Ice in the Alps
Unit 2: Ice in the past
Unit 3: Enquiry: Avalanche!

CHAPTER 7 Water   80
Unit 1: The water cycle
Unit 2: Water supply in Spain
Unit 3: Water pollution

CHAPTER 8 France   91
Unit 1: A tour of France
Unit 2: Energy in France
Unit 3: Champagne
Unit 4: The Camargue

CHAPTER 9 Sweden   108
Unit 1: Getting to know Sweden
Unit 2: The Sami reindeer herders of northern Sweden
Unit 3: Forests in Sweden
Unit 4: Stockholm: European city of culture 1998

Index   124

ICELAND

INARI (CH2)

LAPPLAND (CH9)

PITEA

HELSINKI

TARTAN OIL
RIG (CH5)

OSLO

STOCKHOLM (CH9)

BALTIC SEA

NORTH SEA

COPENHAGEN

River Coquet (CH3)

GREAT LANGDALE (CH3)

DUBLIN

MAIDENHEAD (CH3)

AMSTERDAM
THE HAGUE

BERLIN

AVIARIES FARM (CH4)

LONDON

River Rhine (CH3)

BRUSSELS

LA RANCE (CH8)

LUX.

VIENNA

PARIS

ALPS

GALTÜR (CH6)

CHAMPAGNE
REGION (CH8)

MER DE GLACE (CH6)

SANTIAGO (CH7)

BIESCAS (CH3)

ROME

AEGEAN SEA

PYRENEES

MADRID

LISBON

SEVILLE (CH2)

MEDITERRANEAN SEA

ATHENS

ALMERIA (CH7)

RHODES

CRETE

A sense of place

Geography is about people and places. We need to have a sense of place so that we can understand where places are in relation to one another. This book is about Europe which, of course, includes the United Kingdom. This chapter will help you learn the basic geography of Europe. It will help to give you a sense of place.

1 What is Europe?

1.1 Europe – one of the smallest continents in the World ▶

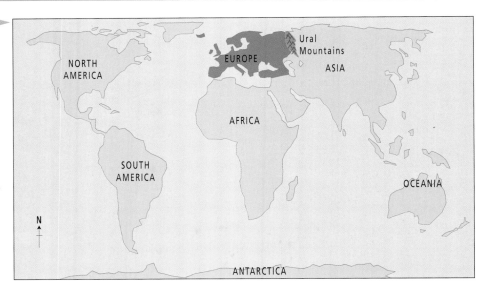

Europe is one of the world's seven continents (see Figure 1.1). Unlike Africa or South America, it is not very easy to know where Europe starts or finishes because it merges into another continent, Asia. The border between Europe and Asia is the Ural Mountains. You can see this mountain range on Figure 1.1.

What is the European Union?

Most of the case studies in this book come from a group of countries called the European Union (Figure 1.2). The **European Union**, or EU as it is commonly known, consists of 15 countries, including the UK.

The European Union is like a club. It started in

1957 when six countries decided that they would all benefit from working more closely together. They signed an agreement called the Treaty of Rome. The six founder members were France, West Germany (at this time, Germany was split into West and East), The Netherlands, Belgium, Italy and Luxembourg. Since that date, other countries have joined, including the UK in 1973 (see Table 1.3). At first, the group of countries was called the European Economic Community (EEC). It was renamed the European Union in 1993.

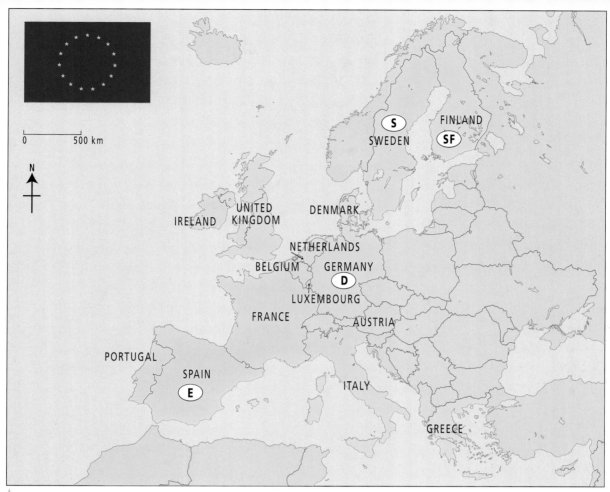

1.2 Members of the European Union, 1999

1.3 The European Union

Date of joining	Countries
1957	France, Germany, Italy, Netherlands, Belgium, Luxembourg
1973	United Kingdom, Denmark, Republic of Ireland
1981	Greece
1986	Spain, Portugal
1995	Austria, Finland, Sweden

What does the EU do?

There is a great deal of co-operation between EU countries. Goods and people can travel freely within its borders. In 1999, a European currency called the **euro**, was introduced to make trading between countries easier. The EU produces guidelines on a whole range of issues including health, hygiene, pollution levels and transport. The EU is also concerned in trying to maintain peace, and in seeking justice throughout the world. Many more countries in eastern Europe want to join.

1 Draw a timeline showing the development of the European Union:

a Using the data in Table 1.3, mark when each country joined.

b Show when the Treaty of Rome was signed.

c Mark the year when the EEC became known as the EU.

d Give your timeline a title: 'The growth of the European Union'.

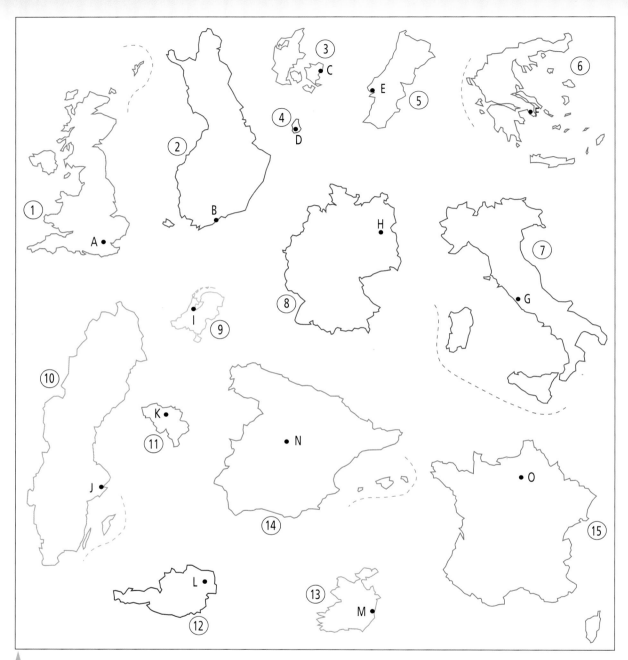

▲ *1.4 European Union – country outlines and capital cities*

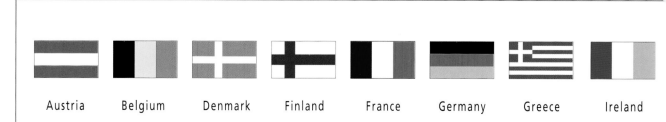

2 Look at Figure 1.2 and Atlas Map A, page 10.
Try to identify the two countries which have chosen not to be members of the EU from the following clues:
- I am surrounded by countries who are all members of the EU. I have no coastline.
- I am part of Scandinavia. I have a long coastline.

3 Look at Figure 1.4. The EU countries have been drawn to scale. Notice how they differ greatly in size from one another.

a Trace the countries labelled 1–15. Then, use Figure 1.2 to identify each country. Put this information in a key below the country outlines.

b Name the capital cities, labelled A–O, on Figure 1.4. Use Atlas Map A, page 10, to help you. Add this information to your key.

4 When a car is in a foreign country, it has an international sign on it. The sign for the United Kingdom is GB. Try to match the following signs to their correct European Union countries (the more difficult ones are shown on Figure 1.2).

5 For this activity you need a blank outline map of Europe. You'll need to refer to Atlas Maps A and B, pages 10–11, as you're going to produce a map showing the basic geography of Europe.

a Use Figure 1.2 to lightly shade the countries of the European Union so that they stand out from the rest of Europe. Use a colour of your choice, but shade very lightly. Add a key to explain the shading.

b Name the shaded countries.

c Mark on and name the capital cities in the EU (these are shown on Figure 1.4). You could show them with letters on the map, and name them in the key if you wish.

d Use Atlas Map A, to locate and name, the other countries and capital cities of Europe on your outline map.

e Now, using a different colour from the one you used earlier, lightly shade: Cyprus, Poland, the Czech Republic, Hungary, Slovenia and Estonia. These countries all hope to join the EU from 2002 onwards. Add this information to your key. (Do you notice anything about the location of these countries?)

f Turn to Atlas Map B and label the following on your map:
- North Sea
- Atlantic Ocean
- Mediterranean Sea.

g Give your map a title: 'Europe – countries, cities and EU membership'.

| Italy | Luxembourg | Netherlands | Portugal | Spain | Sweden | United Kingdom |

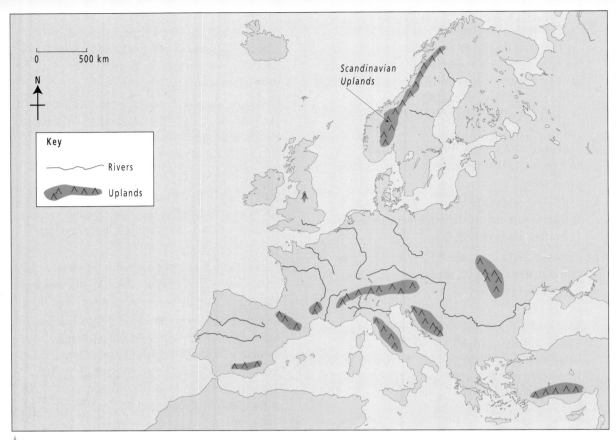

Key

⌇⌇⌇⌇ Rivers

Uplands

Scandinavian
Uplands

0   500 km

N

▲ 1.5 Uplands and rivers of Europe

6 You need another blank outline of Europe for this activity. You are going to produce a map showing the main physical features of Europe.

a Look at Figure 1.5. Copy the upland areas and rivers on to your map. Use colours to make your map clearer and more attractive.

b Label the mountains and rivers. Use Atlas Map B to help you.

c Name the following seas and oceans:
  ● North Sea
  ● Atlantic Ocean
  ● Mediterranean Sea
  ● English Channel
  ● Bay of Biscay
  ● Baltic Sea
  ● Adriatic Sea
  ● Black Sea.

d Give your map a title: ' Uplands, rivers and seas of Europe'.

7 Look at Table 1.6.

a Draw a **choropleth map** (see Skills Box 1, opposite) to show either television ownership or unemployment in the European Union. You could fill in an outline map of Europe. Below is a key that you could follow for television ownership. (Remember, it is the darkness of the colour that counts so, for example, when you change from orange to red, make sure that the red is clearly darker than the orange.)

Television sets (per 1000 pop.)

less than 300	➡	⬜
301–400	➡	🔲
401–500	➡	🔲
501– 600	➡	🔲
more than 601	➡	⬛

b Describe the pattern shown by your map. Is there much variation across Europe? Discuss your findings in groups or as a class.

▼ *1.6 European Union Factfile*

Country	Area (km²)	Population (millions)	Cars (per 1000 pop.)	TVs (per 1000 pop.)	Unemployment (%)
France	544 000	57.2	430	580	11.5
Germany	357 000	81.2	488	560	8.3
Italy	301 046	57.8	518	430	11.9
Netherlands	41 160	15.1	383	540	7.0
Belgium	30 519	10.0	416	450	10.2
Luxembourg	2 586	0.39	567	350	3.9
UK	244 111	57.6	373	430	8.8
Denmark	43 080	5.2	309	530	6.7
Rep. of Ireland	68 900	3.5	242	300	14.4
Greece	131 990	10.2	177	350	8.9
Spain	504 800	39.1	344	400	22.7
Portugal	92 100	9.8	357	300	7.2
Austria	83 855	7.9	433	500	n/a
Finland	388 142	5.0	368	630	17.2
Sweden	449 964	8.8	409	670	9.2

Source: European Commission

SKILLS BOX 1

Choropleth maps

A choropleth map uses different colours or shades to show information. It is a useful way of showing how things are distributed across an area. The map on the right shows a typical choropleth map.

Key points

1 The data is arranged into a number of groups (between 4 and 8 groups is a good number).
2 Each group has a colour, increasing in darkness as the value increases (yellow–orange–red–dark brown–black is a sequence that works well).
3 There is no overlap in values from one group to the next.
4 The groups are usually equal in size.
5 Areas without data are left blank.

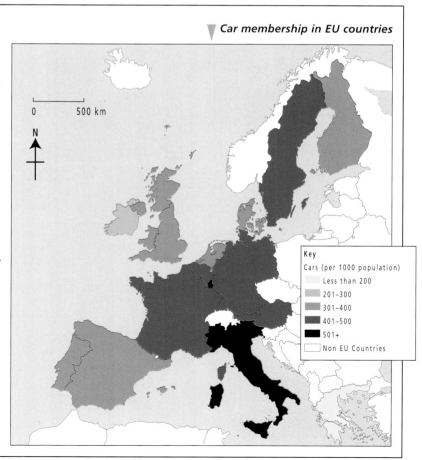

▼ *Car membership in EU countries*

0   500 km

N

Key
Cars (per 1000 population)
☐ Less than 200
▨ 201–300
▨ 301–400
▨ 401–500
■ 501+
☐ Non EU Countries

Atlas Map B

KEY

over 5000 m
3000 - 5000 m
2000 - 3000 m
1000 - 2000 m
500 - 1000 m
200 - 500 m
0 - 200 m
land below sea level

Ice cap

▲ 4808   Mountain height
(height in metres)

Scale 1 : 22 000 000

0   200   400   600   800 km

© Bartholomew Ltd 1999

Weather and climate

Weather and climate vary a great deal in Europe. Some parts of Europe suffer from frequent storms and periods of severe cold, whereas other parts have hot, dry conditions. Weather and climate have a huge effect on people's lives as you will discover in this book.

1 The weather in Europe

The **weather** is the condition of the atmosphere (the air above our heads) over a short period of time. Look at Figure 1.1. Notice in the key that different colours are used to show the temperatures. The hottest areas on the map are shaded purple and the coldest areas are green. Locate the UK on Figure 1.1. How do our temperatures compare to those in the rest of Europe?

It is easy to see, from Figure 1.1, why so many people from the UK go to southern Europe for their summer holiday.

Key
- 10–14°C
- 15–19°C
- 20–24°C
- 25–29°C
- 30–34°C
- Over 34°C
- • Cities

0   500 km

1.1 European temperatures, 4 July 1998 ▶

1.2 European weather, 4 July 1998 ▼

Amsterdam	☁	Dublin	☁	Madrid	☀		☀	Sunny
Athens	☀	Helsinki	⛅	Paris	☀		⛅	Sunny intervals
Berlin	☁	Lisbon	☀	Rome	⛈		☁	Cloudy
Brussels	☁	London	⛅	Stockholm	☁		🌧	Rain
Copenhagen	☁	Luxembourg	⛅	Vienna	🌧		⛈	Thunderstorm

The main reason for the high temperatures in this part of Europe is that in mid-summer the sun is very powerful. In addition, southern Europe is often affected by warm winds that spread north from the Sahara Desert in northern Africa.

Northern Europe is much cooler. This is because in these higher latitudes, the sun is not as high in the sky and therefore not as strong as it is in southern Europe. Also, it is quite common for cooler air from the Arctic to spread south over northern Europe.

Europe's big chill

In early January 1997, much of Europe was affected by icy Arctic conditions which spread down from the north. In some places temperatures fell to minus 10°C. It was even colder than in Greenland! Over 200 people were killed by the extreme cold. In Germany, grave-diggers had to use pneumatic drills to bury the victims in the frozen ground. Figure 1.3 describes some of the effects of the big freeze.

▼ *1.3 Europe's big chill, January 1997*

- Several rivers became frozen, including the Elbe, the Danube and the Loire. The River Thames froze at Marlow near London.
- In Romania, more than 50 people died from the cold.
- Two people died in skiing accidents in Switzerland.
- In Poland, 40 old or homeless people died from the cold.
- In Russia, 300 people were trapped in a tunnel by avalanches.
- Snow caused chaos in Kent.
- Frankfurt airport was closed due to snow.
- In the Netherlands, people skated on frozen canals and rivers.

1 Study Figure 1.1.

a In which temperature band is Scotland?

b In which temperature band is south east England?

c Which country in the following pairs is the warmest.
- Norway or Sweden
- Denmark or Spain
- Ireland or Iceland.

d Suggest two reasons why northern Europe is cooler than southern Europe?

2 You will need an outline map of Europe for this activity.

a Copy the temperature map shown in Figure 1.1 onto your map.

b Look at Table 1.2. Put this information onto your map, using the symbols shown. Use Atlas Map A, page 10, to help you locate the cities.

c Write a few sentences comparing the weather in northern Europe with that in southern Europe.

3 Study Figure 1.3 carefully.

a Find one good thing about the winter weather in Figure 1.3. Can you suggest any other advantages of winter weather?

b In pairs, make a list of problems caused by severe winter weather that are not mentioned in Figure 1.3. Try to think back to last winter.

4 Show the information in Figure 1.3 on an outline map of Europe. Use Atlas Maps A and B, pages 10–11, to help you.

a Draw on the rivers that became frozen in places.

b Locate the countries, the city of Frankfurt in Germany and the county of Kent, to the south east of London.

c Write labels on your map to describe the effects of the winter weather. Don't forget to do your writing in ink and to give your map a title.

2 The climate of Europe

What is climate?

It is important to understand the difference between the weather of a place and its climate. The weather describes the short term, day-to-day conditions such as temperature, cloud cover and rainfall. The **climate** of a place describes the average weather over a number of years. (Climatic information is calculated as an average over a period of 30 years.)

Look at the **climate graph** in Figure 2.1. It plots the details of London's climate for January to April. Notice that there are two lines for **temperature**. The highest temperature is plotted as the maximum temperature, and the lowest as the minimum temperature. **Precipitation**, for example rain and snow, is shown on the same graph but as a series of bars rather than lines.

Patterns of climate in Europe

Figure 2.2 shows the different climates of Europe. In the key, the climate of the UK is described as having 'rain in all months and no extremes of hot or cold'. This may seem strange to you as some months are very dry, and we do get very hot or very cold days. However, remember that climate is measured by averaging weather data over many years. A few heat waves or cold snaps will make little difference to the overall average temperature.

	J	F	M	A	M	J	J	A	S	O	N	D
Max. temp. (°C)	6	7	10	13	17	20	22	21	19	14	10	7
Min. temp. (°C)	2	2	3	6	8	12	14	13	11	8	5	4
Precipitation (mm)	54	40	37	37	46	45	57	59	49	57	64	48

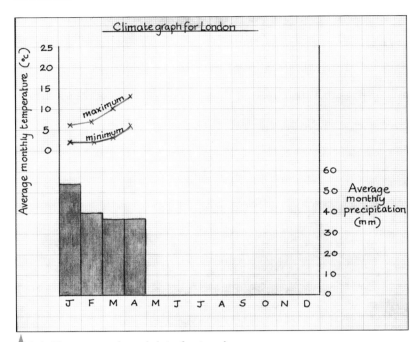

2.1 Climate graph and data for London

1 Draw a climate graph for London, using the data in Figure 2.1. The first part of the graph has been drawn for you. Use the same axes and take care to plot the information accurately.

a Add labels to show:
  ● the month with the highest temperature
  ● the two months with the lowest minimum temperature
  ● the month with the highest precipitation
  ● the two months with the lowest precipitation.

b Work out the total average precipitation for the year.

2 Study Figure 2.2.
a In which climate region is London located?
b How well does the climate graph for London fit the description of its climate given in the key.

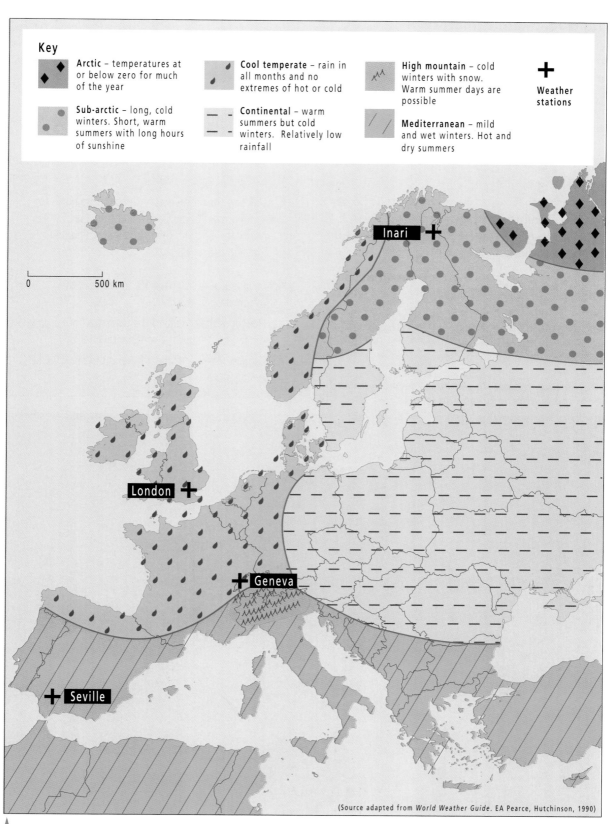

Key

Arctic – temperatures at or below zero for much of the year

Sub-arctic – long, cold winters. Short, warm summers with long hours of sunshine

Cool temperate – rain in all months and no extremes of hot or cold

Continental – warm summers but cold winters. Relatively low rainfall

High mountain – cold winters with snow. Warm summer days are possible

Mediterranean – mild and wet winters. Hot and dry summers

Weather stations

Inari

London

Geneva

Seville

0   500 km

(Source adapted from *World Weather Guide*. EA Pearce, Hutchinson, 1990)

2.2 Europe's climate

The three main climates

The cool, **temperate** climate experienced by western Europe is due to the south-westerly **prevailing winds** (the most common wind direction). These winds bring moist, mild air from the Atlantic, accounting for the high rainfall and lack of extremes of temperature (see Photo 2.3).

In contrast, eastern Europe has a **continental** climate. This is because it is in the centre of a large area of land. Land heats up and cools down much faster than water, so summers tend to be hotter and winters colder than coastal areas. It is also drier than coastal areas, being far away from the moist winds that blow off the sea.

Southern Europe has a **Mediterranean** climate. Summers are hot and dry and winters tend to be mild and wet. Look again at Figure 2.2 to discover more about the climates of Europe.

3 You will need an outline map of Europe.

a Copy Figure 2.2 onto your map. Use colours to show the different climatic regions. Don't forget the key.

b Use Figure 2.2 and Atlas Map A, page 10, to locate and label the following towns and cities :
- Inari (Finland)
- Rome (Italy)
- Stockholm (Sweden)
- Vienna (Austria)
- Berlin (Germany)
- Geneva (Switzerland)
- Dublin (Rep. of Ireland).

c Describe the differences in climate from north to south across Europe. Take a line from Inari in the north, through Stockholm and Berlin, and on to Rome in the south.

4 Look at Figure 2.2, page 15, and re-read the information in this unit.

a How does the climate of the west coast of Europe differ from that of the continental interior?

b Suggest reasons for the differences in rainfall and temperature.

2.3 The cool, temperate climate of western Ireland keeps the landscape green and lush ▼

Does climate matter?

The climate of a place has an important effect on its geography. For example, it influences what type of plants will grow. The crops that thrive in a Mediterranean climate, such as oranges, tomatoes and olives do not grow well in northern European climates because it is too cold. Houses in northern Europe have central heating and lots of insulation to keep the heat in. But houses in the south are designed to be cooler. People living in hot climates often work in the mornings and early evenings, taking a long break in the middle of the day when the sun is at its hottest. Can you think of any other ways that climate affects people's lives? Look at the photos on this page.

5 Copy and complete Table 2.4 to show how climatic conditions can affect people's lives. (A few examples have been filled in for you.) Try to suggest several examples of 'winners' and 'losers' for each climatic condition.

▼ *2.4 How climate affects people's lives*

Climatic conditions	Winners	Losers
Hot, dry summers.		
Cold winters with lots of snow.	*People who enjoy skiing*	
Mild throughout the year with rain in all months.	*Good for farmers as crops grow well*	
Mild winters with little rain.		

◀ *2.5 Climate affects the way that people live. In southern Europe, school children take a long mid-day break returning to school in the late afternoon.*

▼ *In northern Europe, daylight hours in winter are short and snowfall sometimes makes it difficult for children to get to school.*

3 Enquiry: Mediterranean and sub-Arctic climates

You can use the information in this Enquiry to produce your own project comparing these two very different European climates. Alternatively, you can work through the activities at the end. Try to use a mixture of writing, maps, drawings and diagrams.

ENQUIRY A

Mediterranean climate

In a **Mediterranean** climate the summers tend to be hot and dry. The sun is high in the sky and is very powerful. In some months there is hardly any rainfall and conditions become dry and dusty. In the winter the climate is generally mild and frost-free. However, cold spells do occur and snow may fall in places. Most of the rain falls in the winter (see Table 3.1 below).

Adapting to the climate

Plants and animals that live in a Mediterranean climate have to be able to cope with the hot, dry summers. In some years, long dry spells lead to droughts. Shrubs and bushes grow well. This type of vegetation is called maquis. **Maquis** plants survive the hot, dry conditions because they have long roots that reach deep down into the water below ground. Their small leaves also help to reduce water loss (see Figure 3.2).

Rabbits and ground squirrels are common wild animals. Sheep and goats graze the grasslands (see Photo 3.3).

People often work in the mornings and early evenings to avoid the heat of the midday sun. The Mediterranean climate attracts millions of tourists from cooler countries, seeking heat and sunshine.

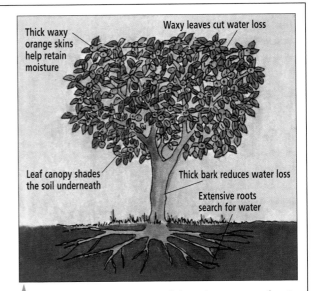

Waxy leaves cut water loss
Thick waxy orange skins help retain moisture
Leaf canopy shades the soil underneath
Thick bark reduces water loss
Extensive roots search for water

3.2 An orange tree – surviving the summer heat

3.3 A typical Mediterranean scene – sheep grazing near a small mountain farmhouse

▼ *3.1 Climate data for Seville (Spain)*

	J	F	M	A	M	J	J	A	S	O	N	D
Max. temp. (°C)	15	17	20	24	27	32	36	36	32	26	20	16
Min. temp. (°C)	6	7	9	11	13	17	20	20	18	14	10	7
Precipitation (mm)	66	61	90	57	41	8	1	5	19	70	67	79

ENQUIRY B

Sub-Arctic climate

In a **sub-Arctic** climate the winters are long, and the summers short. Snow begins to fall in October and may last through to May. For much of the winter it is dark and extremely cold, with as little as two hours of sunlight a day. In midsummer the sun shines day and night and there is no darkness. These long hours of sunshine can lead to quite high temperatures. Precipitation, which is low, occurs in all months – in the winter it is in the form of snow (see Table 3.4).

Adapting to the climate

The long, cold winters make life difficult in a sub-Arctic climate (see Photo 3.5). Plants stop growing. There is little food for wild animals. Deer, beavers and brown bears have thick coats to keep warm. The Arctic hare has huge feet so that it can move over snow easily (Figure 3.6). Its coat changes from brown to white in the winter so that it can hide from predators. People have to dress warmly in the winter because frostbite can be a problem. The long hours of darkness can be unpleasant too. In the summer, mosquitoes are a common pest, especially near lakes and rivers.

3.5 Reindeer in sub-Arctic Norway

3.6 An Arctic hare

▼ *3.4 Climate data for Inari (Finland)*

	J	F	M	A	M	J	J	A	S	O	N	D
Max. temp. (°C)	–9	–9	–3	2	8	14	17	15	9	1	–4	–8
Min. temp. (°C)	–18	–17	–14	–9	0	6	9	7	3	–3	–10	–18
Precipitation (mm)	38	30	25	35	42	48	76	75	57	57	49	41

You will need an outline map of Europe for this activty.

1 Using information from Figure 2.2, page 15, show the distribution of the two types of climate on your map. Use Atlas Map A, page 10, to name the countries influenced by each climate and locate and label some towns and cities. Give your map a title.

2 Draw graphs to compare the climates of Seville and Inari (look at Figure 2.1, page 14, if you need help). Add labels to show the main features of the climates.

3 Read the information about the two climates and compare them. What are the summers like? What's it like in the winter? Does the amount and type of precipitation differ?

4 What conditions do plants and animals have to deal with in the two climates? How do they cope?

5 How are people's lives affected by the two climates? What are the problems? Are there any advantages? Which climate would you prefer to live in? Why?

Further information

● Visit a library – look for books on Weather and Climate with information on these two climates. Also, find wildlife books which tell you how plants and animals have adapted to living in Mediterranean and sub-Arctic conditions.

● Try to access CD–ROM encyclopedias such as Encarta.

Rivers

Much of our landscape has been shaped by rivers. Rivers begin high up in hills and mountains. They flow down to lakes or to the sea. On their way, they carve out valleys and create many landscape features. Rivers can be managed by people to provide such things as transport, water and electricity. Occasionally, rivers may flood, killing people and destroying homes.

1 River study: The Coquet, Northumberland, UK

The River Coquet is over 70 km long. Its **source** (the start of a river) is high up in the Cheviot Hills and its **mouth** (end of a river) is on the coast at Amble, where it flows into the North Sea. Look at the map in Figure 1.2. Notice that there are lots of smaller rivers that join the main river channel. These are called **tributaries**. The land that the river and its tributaries drains is called its **drainage basin**.

2 Look at Photos A–D in Figure 1.2.

a How does the size of the river change downstream?

b How does the size and shape of the river valley change downstream?

c How does the land use either side of the river change downstream?

1 Study the map in Figure 1.2.

a Match each term, labelled A–F, with its correct definition below.

A Drainage basin D Confluence
B Source E Mouth
C Tributary F Meander

– the point where two rivers join

– where a river joins the sea

– the start of a river

– the area drained by a river

– a sweeping bend in a river

– a small stream that joins a larger river

b Make a copy of the river pattern shown in Figure 1.1. Write the labels, A – F, in the correct places.

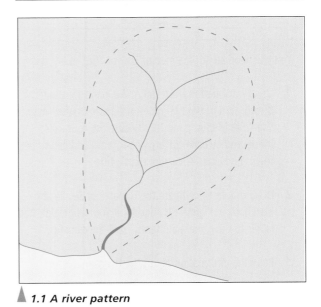

1.1 A river pattern

1.2 The River Coquet ▶

A   *These are the Cheviot Hills. Many streams join together to form the River Coquet. Much of the land is used for farming.*

B   *The river is flowing through a wide and flat valley. The lakes are old gravel pits. In the distance the river bends – these bends are called meanders.*

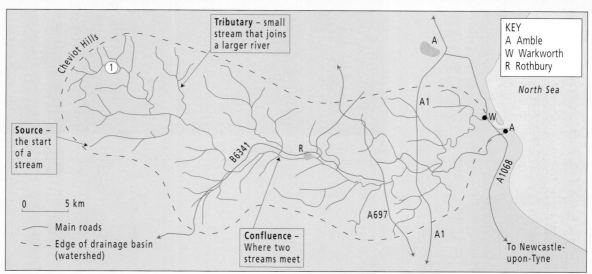

Tributary – small stream that joins a larger river

Source – the start of a stream

Confluence – Where two streams meet

Cheviot Hills

KEY
A Amble
W Warkworth
R Rothbury

North Sea

To Newcastle-upon-Tyne

0   5 km

—— Main roads

– – – Edge of drainage basin (watershed)

C   *This is the town of Warkworth. It was built on land inside a large meander. You can see that much of the surrounding area is ploughed for farming.*

D   *The river is wider now as it joins the sea. This is the mouth of the River Coquet. The town is Amble. Can you see the harbour and the sailing boats?*

River features

1 Valleys

There is heavy rainfall in the Cheviot Hills and the ground is often very wet and boggy. The wettest areas are in small hollows in the hillside (see Photo 1.3). Notice the tall grasses and wildflowers growing in the wet soil. There is a small stream flowing through, but you cannot see it because it is hidden by the grasses. The tiny streams that flow downhill from these hollows, join together to form the River Coquet.

Streams and rivers cut into the ground and carry away soil and fragments of rock. This process is called **erosion**. Photo 1.4 shows how the River Coquet has carved a valley into the landscape.

▲ *1.3 The source of the River Coquet*

▲ *1.4 The valley carved out by the River Coquet. Notice that the shape of the valley is like the letter 'V'. River valleys are sometimes called V-shaped valleys as they often have this shape.*

1.5 A small waterfall on the River Coquet

2 Waterfalls

There are many small **waterfalls** on the River Coquet (see Photo 1.5). Waterfalls often form when a river flows over a tough band of rock. At the point where the tough rock meets softer rock, the river starts to erode more deeply and a step is formed. It is the water tumbling over this step that forms a waterfall. Figure 1.6 shows what happens.

3 Look at the information on waterfalls.

a What is a waterfall?

b Look at Photo 1.5. How is the river different above and below the waterfall?

c Use Figure 1.6 to help you draw a diagram to explain how a waterfall may form.

d Waterfalls are popular attractions. Why do you think people like to visit them? Can you name two famous waterfalls?

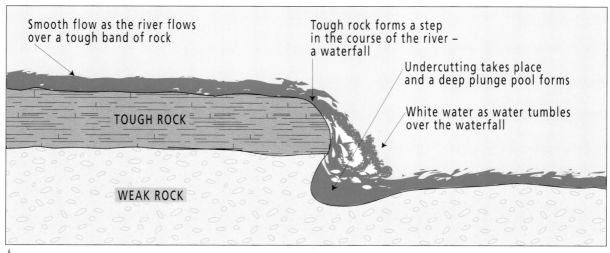

1.6 The formation of a waterfall

23

RIVERS

3 Meanders

The sweeping curves, found in most rivers, are called **meanders**. Photo 1.7 shows a meander in a small tributary as it joins the River Coquet, near Rothbury (see Figure 1.2, page 21, to locate the town of Rothbury).

The photo was taken in the summer when the river was very low. There is not much water in the river channel at this time of year. Notice that one bank has been undercut by erosion. The other bank is made up of sand and pebbles deposited by the river at times of higher flow. Now study Figure 1.8 to discover what happens at a meander.

1.7 A meander ▶

4 Look at the information on meanders.

a What does the word meander mean? Do you think it is a good name for a bend in a river? Why?

b Make a copy of the cross-section in Figure 1.9.

c Add the following labels:
- River cliff
- Undercutting by river erosion
- Deposition by the river
- Point bar

d Use an arrow to show the position of the fastest flow of water. You will need to look carefully at Figure 1.8 for this.

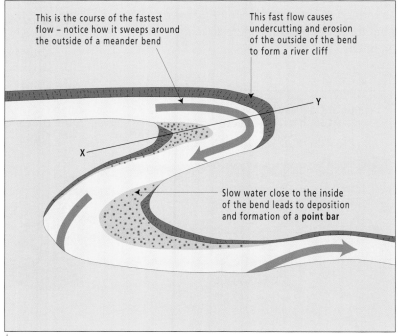

This is the course of the fastest flow – notice how it sweeps around the outside of a meander bend

This fast flow causes undercutting and erosion of the outside of the bend to form a river cliff

Y

X

Slow water close to the inside of the bend leads to deposition and formation of a **point bar**

1.8 Water flow and features of a meandering river

1.10 River features ▶

▲ *1.9 Cross-section across a meander (X–Y on Figure 1.8)*

5 Make a copy of Figure 1.10. Add the following labels in the correct places:
- Meander
- V-shaped valley
- River cliff
- Waterfall
- Source
- Point bar.

OS map and photo study

Figure 1.12 is a map extract of the same stretch of river shown in Photo 1.11. The village of

Thropton is just a few miles west of Rothbury (see Figure 1.2, page 21). The photo was taken above grid reference 005020. Locate this point on the map extract.

6 Refer to Photo 1.11 and Figure 1.12 to answer the following questions.

a In which direction is the photo looking?

b What is the name of the village in the far distance of the photo?

c What is the number of the road that you can see running to the left of the river, towards the village?

d What is the name of the tributary that joins the River Coquet in the village shown in the photo?

e How can you tell from the map that the river is meandering over flat ground?

f Look in grid square 0201. What spot height gives us an idea of how high the river is above sea level?

7 Find the lakes in grid square 0001 (They are not shown on the photo.) These lakes are flooded gravel quarries and they are now a nature reserve.

a Do you think it was a good idea to turn them into lakes, or should the quarries have been filled in? Why?

b Most of the land in the photo is being farmed. Look for ploughed fields and fields with young crops growing in them. What does this suggest about the fertility of the soil on the valley floor?

8 Using Figure 1.12, draw a sketch map showing some of the main features of the river and its valley. Follow the steps below.

a In pencil, draw a grid with the same number of squares as in Figure 1.12. Make each grid 4 cm x 4 cm so that you are doubling its size. Write the gridline numbers at the sides of your map.

b Using the map extract as a guide, carefully draw the River Coquet and its tributaries. Also show the flooded gravel quarries.

c Draw the 90 m and the 100 m contours. These show the width of the valley floor.

d Mark on the following spot heights:
- 185 m (grid square 0302)
- 128 m (grid square 0103)
- 113 m (grid square 0102)

e Draw the main road and number it. Locate the village and name it.

f Complete your map:
- Use colours if you wish
- Label as many features as you can
- Add a scale and a north point
- Give your map a title.

9 Draw a cross-section across the valley of the River Coquet. Start at the 128 m spot height, in grid square 0103, and finish at the 130 m contour, in grid square 0101. Use pencil to begin with and, only use ink and coloured pencils at the end. Follow the steps below.

a With a ruler, draw a straight pencil line between these points. This is your line of section.

b Place a piece of rough paper along the line of section and mark off the contours. Make sure you write the correct values alongside each one.

c Mark the position of the River Coquet, the Wreigh Burn and the B6341.

d Use a graph similar to Figure 1.13 and complete your section by plotting the values.

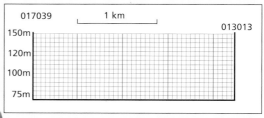

1.13

e Add labels to show the following features. (You may wish to use a key as the cross section is very small!)
- the River Coquet
- the valley of the Coquet
- the flat valley bottom – this is called the floodplain
- the Wreigh Burn tributary
- the B6341.

f Write the grid references above each axis and give your diagram a title.

▲ 1.11 The River Coquet, near Thropton

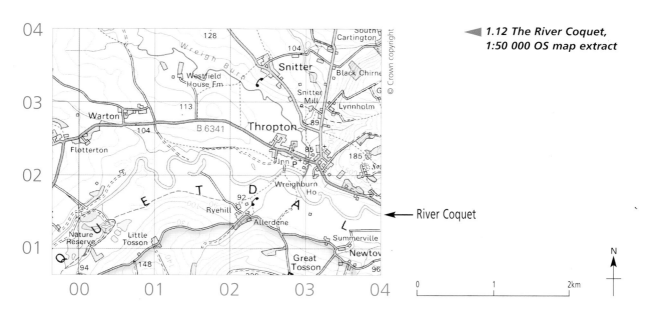

◄ 1.12 The River Coquet,
1:50 000 OS map extract

← River Coquet

2 Managing the River Rhine

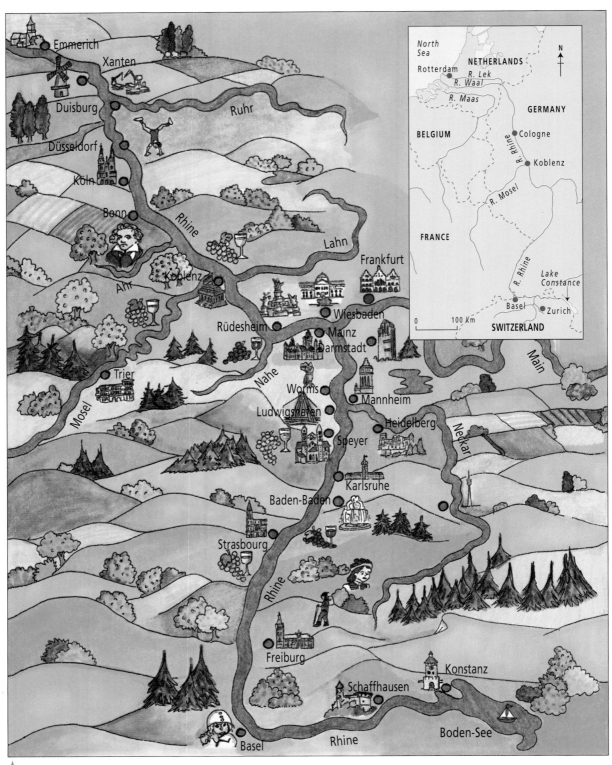

Map labels:

Emmerich, Xanten, Ruhr, Duisburg, Düsseldorf, Köln, Bonn, Rhine, Koblenz, Ahr, Lahn, Frankfurt, Rüdesheim, Wiesbaden, Mainz, Darmstadt, Nahe, Trier, Worms, Mannheim, Mosel, Ludwigshafen, Speyer, Heidelberg, Neckar, Karlsruhe, Baden-Baden, Main, Strasbourg, Rhine, Freiburg, Konstanz, Schaffhausen, Basel, Rhine, Boden-See

Inset map labels:

North Sea, NETHERLANDS, Rotterdam, R. Lek, R. Waal, R. Maas, BELGIUM, GERMANY, Cologne, R. Rhine, Koblenz, R. Mosel, FRANCE, R. Rhine, Lake Constance, Basel, Zurich, SWITZERLAND, N, 0 100 km

2.1 The River Rhine flows for over 850 km through Germany

2.2 Stahlbeck Castle is one of many castles that line the River Rhine. Can you see the vineyards and the barges on the river?

The River Rhine is Europe's third longest river after the Danube and the Volga. It flows for 1320 km from its source in Switzerland to the North Sea in the Netherlands (see inset map in Figure 2.1).

In contrast with the River Coquet, the Rhine cannot be described as a 'natural' river. It has been widened, deepened, dammed and straightened, by people over the years. The river is used for transporting goods and generating electricity. Much work has been done to reduce the risk of flooding. Many large cities are situated on the river including Mannheim, Koblenz, Bonn and Cologne. Its valley slopes are lined with vineyards (see Photo 2.2).

Let's look in more detail at how and why the River Rhine has been managed.

---

1 Study the maps in Figure 2.1.

a Through which two countries, apart from Germany, does the River Rhine flow?

b The Rhine splits into two rivers when it enters the Netherlands. Name the two rivers.

c Into which sea does the Rhine finally flow?

d What symbol is used on Figure 2.1 to show that there are vineyards alongside the Rhine? (Vineyards are where grapes are grown for wine-making.)

e Which tributary river joins the Rhine at Mainz?

f Near which city do the rivers Mosel and Lahn join the Rhine?

2 Study Photo 2.2 and read its caption carefully

a Are the river valley slopes in the photo gentle or steep?

b What is the name given to a valley shaped like this?

c Where in the valley are the roads and the settlements? Why do you think they have been built here?

d Describe the land use in the valley.

e Why do you think the castle was built here?

3 Now make a simple sketch of Photo 2.2. Label the following features:
- River Rhine
- Steep valley slopes
- Main roads
- Barges
- Terraced vineyards.
- Stahlbeck Castle

Transport on the Rhine

Germany's early industrial growth started when large amounts of coal were found near the River Ruhr (see Figure 2.1, page 28). Northern Germany rapidly became a centre for heavy industries such as steel-making. The Rhine was used to transport coal and other raw materials to and from the new industries.

Today the Rhine is one of the world's most important rivers for transporting goods. Over 10 000 ships (mostly barges like those in Photo 2.2) carry over 250 million tonnes of goods on the river every year. The main goods carried are those that are bulky and expensive to transport by road, such as rocks, scrap metal, and coal (see Figure 2.3).

The river channel has been straightened in places to help boats navigate the river more quickly. It has also been deepened to allow larger ships to use the river.

River transport can be very environmentally-friendly as it takes traffic off the roads. This reduces fuel consumption. Emissions from ships are less damaging than exhaust fumes. However, fuel leaks do occur on the river and the wash (waves made by the ships) can damage the river banks.

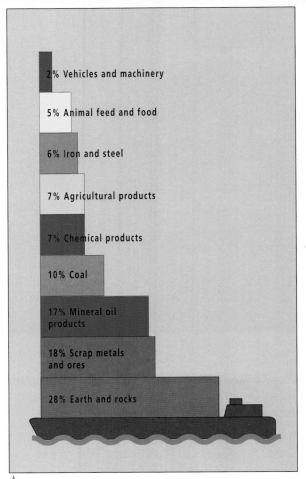

2.3 Freight carried on the River Rhine in a year, shown in percentages

2% Vehicles and machinery
5% Animal feed and food
6% Iron and steel
7% Agricultural products
7% Chemical products
10% Coal
17% Mineral oil products
18% Scrap metals and ores
28% Earth and rocks

4 Study Figure 2.3.

a Choose two words from below to describe the type of freight carried.
light   bulky   compact   small   clean   heavy

b What is the main type of freight?

c On graph paper, present the information in Figure 2.3 as a **proportional bar**. (Look at Figure 3.4 and Question 4, page 50, if you need help).

5 Some people think that more freight should be carried on rivers such as the River Rhine, rather than on the roads.

a What are the advantages of river transport?

b Can you think of any disadvantages of river transport?

Generating electricity

The gradient of much of the Upper Rhine is very steep. The water flows fast and it is used to generate **hydro-electric power** (HEP). Most of the HEP stations are found along the 180 km stretch between Lake Constance and Basle (see Figure 2.1, page 28).

A series of 13 dams, called a staircase, has been built on the river to generate electricity. Look at Figure 2.4 to see how each dam raises the level of the water upstream. This creates a head of water above the dam so that the water will flow faster as it passes through the turbines. The turbines convert the power of the water into electrical power. Notice that each dam has a lock to allow ships to pass through.

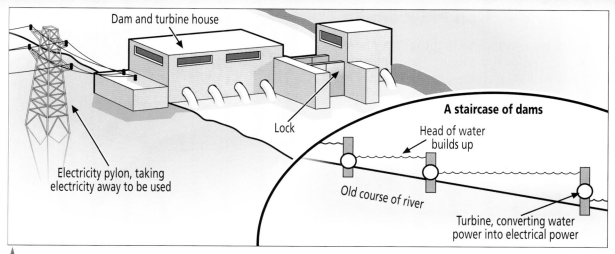

▲ *2.4 Generating hydro-electric power on the Rhine, near Basle*

6 Study Figure 2.4. Describe how people manage the Upper Rhine to generate electricity. Draw simple diagrams to help you.

Pollution

The River Rhine used to be called the 'sewer of Europe'. This is because it was badly polluted, particularly during the 1960s and 1970s. There were several causes of the pollution:

- Heavy industries along the river, released waste into it. The waste often contained damaging heavy metals like mercury.

- Farm chemicals, from fertilisers and pesticides, were washed into the river. These chemicals encouraged the growth of algae. The algae took valuable oxygen from the river water, causing fish and plant life to die.

- Salts were washed in from mines close to the river. They polluted the river even more.

In 1986, a fire in a chemical factory near Basle led to the most serious pollution incident on the Rhine. Thirty tonnes of highly toxic (poisonous) chemicals, used in making dyes and pesticides, spilled into the river. Over half a million fish died, and the Rhine ecosystem was severely affected (Photo 2.5). The water supply in towns and villages nearby had to be switched off.

▲ *2.5 Chemicals can pollute rivers for many years before they disperse*

The Rhine Action Programme

After this, people decided that the river must be cleaned up. In 1987, the Rhine Action Programme was launched. New waste-water treatment plants were built to process industrial waste before it reached the river. In addition, farmers were encouraged to use less chemicals on their land. River quality improved in the 1990s and the first salmon, for many years, were caught.

2.6 Salmon can only live in unpolluted rivers

7 Read the section on pollution, page 31.

a Design a poster to tell industries and farmers, based along the Rhine, not to pollute the river. Make it as dramatic as you can.

b How would you have felt if you had lived in a village affected by the pollution incident of 1986? Write a letter to a friend, explaining what happened and how you felt. Use Photo 2.5 to help you.

c What were the two key things that the Rhine Action Programme did to improve the quality of the river water? Are there any signs that the River Rhine is less polluted now?

3 Flooding!

Flood in the Spanish Pyrenees

In August 1996, a **flash flood** sent torrents of water, mud, rocks and uprooted trees, through a campsite in the mountains of northern Spain (Photo 3.1). Over 60 people were killed and nearly 200 injured.

The flood followed two days of heavy rain and thunderstorms. Many small streams, flowing down the mountainside, became swollen and some burst their banks. The small stream that ran through the campsite (see Figure 3.2) became a river of mud, over two metres deep, in just a few seconds.

3.1 Disaster in the Pyrenees

What went wrong?

A bridge above the campsite became blocked by broken tree trunks during the storms. Water collected behind the bridge and eventually, the bridge gave way. All the water that had built up behind the bridge poured through the campsite. Figure 3.3 gives an eye-witness account of what happened.

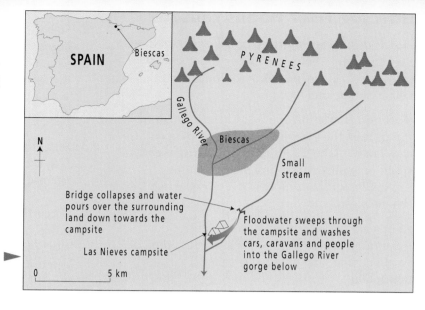

3.2 Details of the flash flood that hit Las Nieves campsite in northern Spain

▼ *3.3 Barry Copestake and his wife Andree's ordeal was reported in a local newspaper*

It was absolute chaos...

Barry Copestake, a teacher from Grimsby, and his wife Andree were lucky to survive the flood. Here is their story, as told by Barry.

'It's a great campsite, a beautiful place. It's surrounded by mountains. It was raining for about two hours and really got bad towards the end. I heard someone screaming. I looked out of the tent and I could see water cascading down the side of the campsite just outside...'

'...We decided to get into the car and go, but it was too late. We got about ten yards and it [the torrent of water] just ripped through the campsite. It turned the car over and everything went black. We travelled upside down in the water for several hundred yards and we came to rest upside down against a caravan stuck by some trees. It was absolute chaos. There were stones, trees, caravans and cars piled up and people wandering about in shock. It was terrible.'

---

1 Choose one of the following activities:

a You are a radio reporter who has just arrived on the scene (see Photo 3.1). Write a short report, describing what you can see. As your report is for the radio, try to be as descriptive as you can.

b Create a newspaper front page describing the flood, its causes and its effects. Try to present the information in a way that would attract people to read it – maybe starting with a dramatic headline and photo, followed by extracts from Barry Copestake's account (Figure 3.3) and a diagram to show what happened.

How are river floods caused?

Floods occur when there is too much water for a river channel to hold. The excess water simply spills over the river's banks and floods the neighbouring land (see photo 3.4).

Most floods, like the one that swept through the campsite in the Pyrenees, are caused by very heavy rain. In the UK, floods often occur in early spring when heavy rain and melting snows combine to produce more water than the river channels can hold.

Floods are perfectly natural river events. Some rivers flood two or three times a year, building up an area of flat land either side called a **floodplain**.

Developing floodplains

When a river floods it leaves behind a layer of silt. The silt develops into a very fertile soil, which explains why floodplains are widely used for farming. As floodplains are flat, they are easy to develop for housing, industry, and transport networks, such as roads and railways.

The use of floodplains by people, increases the dangers associated with flooding. When a river floods and there is a town on its floodplain, many people's lives will be affected.

---

2 Read the information on how river floods are caused. Write a short paragraph, include the following points:
- a definition of a flood
- the most common cause of flooding
- how melting snow increases the risk of flooding.

3 Study Photo 3.4. Work in pairs to make a list of the likely effects of the flooding. Consider both short term and longer term effects.

4 Flooding is a hazard when people live and work on floodplains. Give two reasons why early settlers might have decided to live on a floodplain. Should development of floodplains be controlled?

▲ *3.4 Flooding can cause a lot of damage in towns which are built on the floodplain of a river*

How can floods be prevented?

There are a number of ways in which the risk of flooding can be reduced. Here are four methods which are commonly used:

- Planting trees in the river basin. The trees act as a break on rainfall and reduce the amount of rain reaching the ground. Trees also use up water as they grow.

- River channels are made larger by dredging so that they can hold more water (see Photo 3.5).

- Walls called **flood embankments** are built to increase the height of the river channel (see Photo 3.6).

- **Flood relief (by-pass) channels** can be built around towns. They divert excess water out of rivers and reduce the risk of flooding.

5 Look at Photo 3.5.

a Describe what is happening.

b How does dredging help to stop flooding?

c How do the embankments shown in Photo 3.6 help to stop flooding?

▼ *3.5 A river being dredged*

▲ *3.6 Flood relief channels like this in York have been built in towns in northern Europe*

Flood protection at Maidenhead, UK

Maidenhead is located alongside the River Thames in Berkshire, to the west of London. For years it has suffered from floods. In 1947 and, more recently in 1990, many homes were damaged by floodwater and several roads were impassable. A severe flood in the future could cause an estimated £40 million worth of damage!

To solve the problem, engineers are building a flood relief channel. This will take away some of the water which might otherwise cause the River Thames to burst its banks. Figure 3.7 outlines the scheme.

The Environment Agency, whose job it is to protect areas from flooding, want to create an attractive new channel. It will be lined with trees and plants to make it look as natural as possible. There will be footpaths, picnic areas and a specially designed disabled persons' fishing area. Figure 3.8 shows what the channel may look like.

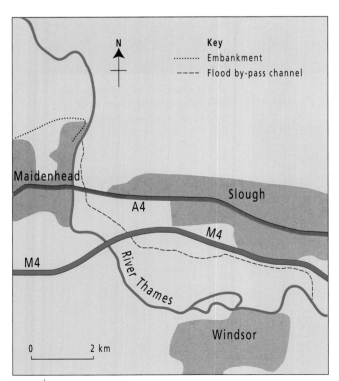

▲ 3.7 Maidenhead flood relief channel

6 Look at the section on flood protection at Maidenhead.

a Why has it been decided to protect Maidenhead from future flooding?

b How will the flood relief channel solve the problem?

c Work out the length of the food relief channel by using the scale on Figure 3.7.

d Alongside which major road will the relief channel run?

e Will the relief channel be to the north or south of the River Thames?

f What other measure will help protect Maidenhead?

7 Look at Figure 3.8.

a Describe what the flood relief channel will look like.

b Does the scene appeal to you? Why?

c What else will be provided for the local people?

d Can you suggest other attractions that could be added to make the local people more likely to welcome the new channel?

8 Some local people are not in favour of the flood relief channel. The Environment Agency has asked you to design a leaflet, to be delivered to people in Maidenhead, describing the benefits of the scheme. Use maps and sketches to produce an attractive leaflet to promote the scheme.

▲ 3.8 Maidenhead flood relief channel – a vision of the future?

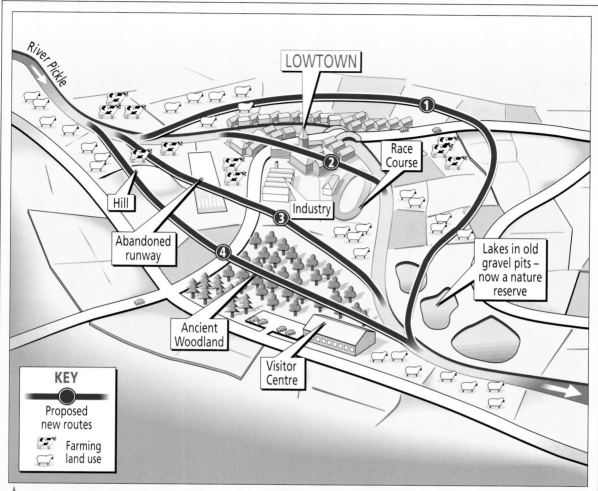

River Pickle

LOWTOWN

①

Race Course

②

Hill

③ Industry

Abandoned runway

④

Lakes in old gravel pits – now a nature reserve

Ancient Woodland

Visitor Centre

KEY

Proposed new routes

Farming land use

▲ *3.9 A flood relief channel for Lowtown*

9 Study Figure 3.9. The small town of Lowtown has been flooded several times over the last few years. It has been decided to build a flood relief channel to take some of the water out of the river. Notice that four possible routes are shown on Figure 3.9.

a Which route is the longest?

b Which route is the shortest?

c Which route runs through part of Lowtown?

d Route 4 has just been rejected. Can you think of two reasons why?

e You have been asked to select the best route for the flood relief channel. Look carefully at the remaining routes 1, 2, and 3. Which route do you think is best? Write a few sentences saying why you think your route is better than the other two.

Web search

There is an enormous amount of information on the Internet about flooding. Carry out a search using a search engine such as Yahoo. You could search for information about a recent flood event. There are many organisations in the United States such as the National Oceanic and Atmospheric Administration (NOAA) and the Federal Emergency Management Agency (FEMA). Try the National Climatic Data Center at www.ncdc.noaa.gov/

The International Federation of the Red Cross, www.ifrc.org/news/sitreps/

has reports on recent floods throughout the world.

Farming

Farming is an example of a primary industry. Farmers plough the land to grow cereals, such as wheat and barley, and vegetables. They rear animals for meat and milk. Farmers also help to preserve the countryside for us all to enjoy. There are many different types of farming in Europe as you will discover in this chapter.

1 The farm system

The **farm system** is a way of looking at what happens on a farm. Firstly, we can identify a number of **inputs** such as the weather, the land, the machines and the workers. Then we can consider the farming activities or **processes** that are carried out, such as milking, ploughing or repairing fences. Finally, we can see the **outputs** from the farm system such as milk and crops. Look at Figure 1.2, opposite, which shows some examples of inputs, processes and outputs.

Figure 1.1 What happens on a farm

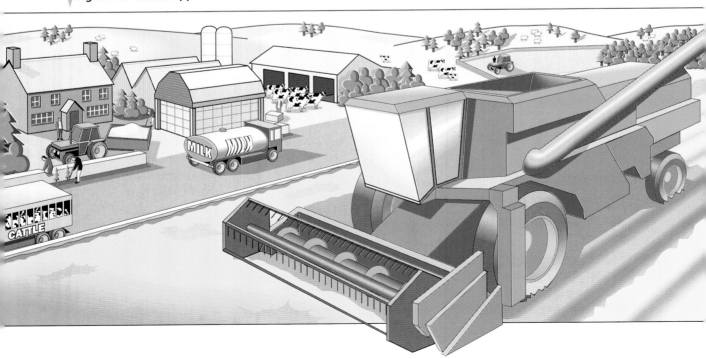

1 Study Figure 1.2, below

a In rough, try to list as many inputs, processes (farming activities) and outputs that you can from Figure 1.2.

b Now, work with a neighbour or as a class, to list other farming inputs, processes and outputs.

c To present your lists, draw a diagram similar to Figure 1.2, on page 39. Write your examples of inputs, processes and outputs in the correct places. Use simple sketches and colour to make your diagram interesting to look at.

Figure 1.2 The farm system

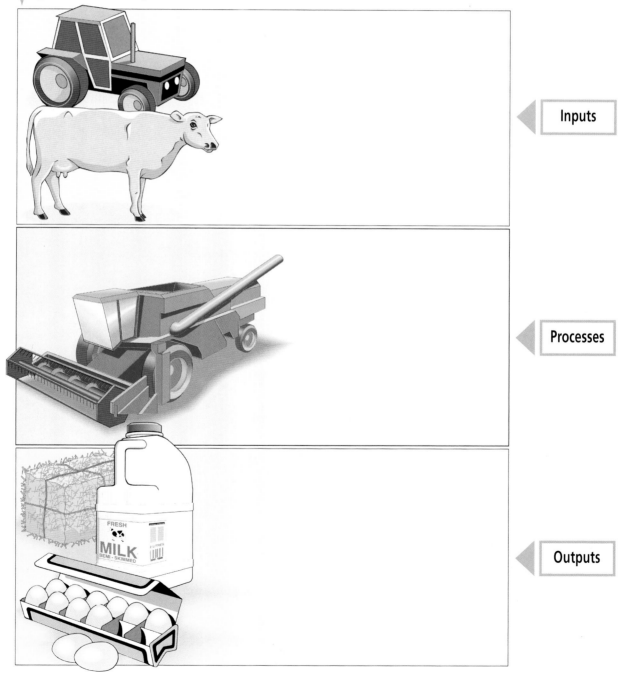

Inputs

Processes

Outputs

2 Farming case study: Aviaries Farm, UK

Aviaries Farm is a large farm located near the town of Wincanton in Somerset (see Figure 2.1). It is an **organic** farm. Unlike most farms in the UK, organic farms do not use chemicals to fertilise the soil or to kill pests. They also avoid using medicines and hormones on their livestock. (Non-organic farms will use all these things to increase their yields and cut their costs.)

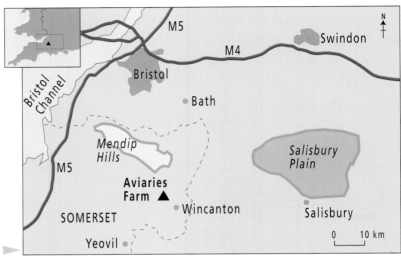

2.1 The location of Aviaries Farm ▶

▲ *2.2 Aerial view of Aviaries Farm*

2.3 Mr Dowding: 'I decided to go organic because I was concerned that farmers were using too many chemicals and artificial fertilisers, threatening the health of the land, the animals and people who eat the food.'

About the farm

Aviaries Farm is over 400 hectares in size (one hectare is about twice the size of a football field). Look at the gently rolling landscape around the farm on Photo 2.2. This is good land for farming, although the soils are not very rich. The amount of rainfall is ideal for growing grass.

The farmer, Mr Dowding, relies heavily on machinery to do the work on the farm. There is a modern milking parlour for the twice-daily milking of the cows (see Photo 2.4). He also has a combine harvester to cut the wheat and seven tractors (see Photo 2.5). He employs six people full time to help him run the farm and several people part time, especially in the summer, to help with all the weeding. Weeds are a major problem because, being an organic farm, Mr Dowding cannot use chemicals to control them.

2.4 The milking parlour at Aviaries Farm

> **1** Aviaries Farm is an organic farm.
>
> **a** What does this mean?
>
> **b** What problem does the farmer have to cope with in the summer? How does he overcome this problem?
>
> **c** Look at Photo 2.3. Why did Mr Dowding decide to farm organically?
>
> **d** Do you think organic farming is a good idea? Explain your answer.

2.5 Using a tractor to plant potatoes

OS mapwork study

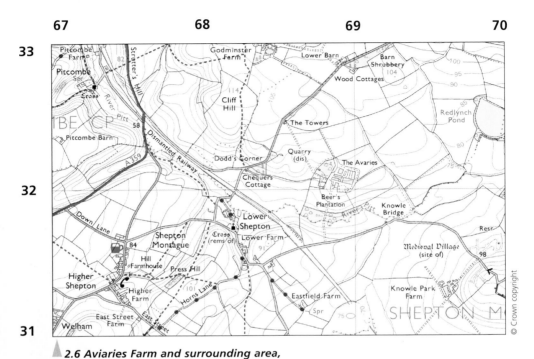

2.6 Aviaries Farm and surrounding area, 1:25 000 OS map extract

© Crown copyright

2 Study the map extract in Figure 2.6.

a What is the six-figure grid reference of Aviaries Farm (it is labelled 'The Avaries' on the map)?

b Mr Dowding lives at Hill Farm House in Shepton Montague. What is the four-figure grid reference of Hill Farm House?

c How far apart are the two farms to the nearest 100 metres?

d In which direction is Aviaries Farm from Hill Farm House? Is it north, south west, west, north east, or south east?

e Look carefully at the contour values around the farm.

- What is the approximate height above sea level of the farm?

- Is the land sloping to the north or to the south?

f What is the name of the river that flows to the south of Aviaries Farm?

g What is the name of the woodland to the south of Aviaries Farm?

h Use the key, to find out what type of wood is found just to the north west of Aviaries Farm.

——— A 35 ———	Main road
———————	Secondary roads
———·········	Track
··················	Path
- - - - - - - -	Footpath
• • •	Public access route
80 95 110 125	Contours
～～～	River
🌲🌲 🌲	Coniferous trees
🌳🌳	Non-coniferous trees
🌲🌳 🌲🌳	Mixed Woodland
Spr	Spring
⛪	Place of worship
☎	Public telephone
🍺	Public house

Mixed farming – cattle and crops

Aviaries Farm is a **mixed farm**. This means that it grows crops as well as rearing animals.

Mr Dowding has 285 cows which produce milk. For most of the year, they are kept outdoors where they graze in the fields. They are taken to the farm twice a day to be milked. In the winter, when the weather is poor and the grass stops growing, the cattle are brought to the farm where they live in cattle yards and sheds. They are fed with concentrated food that is bought, together with some of the crops grown on the farm.

Food crops that are grown to be fed to animals are called **fodder crops**. The most important fodder crop is grass. Fields of grass are cut several times a year (see Photo 2.7). The cut grass is stored in a pit where it turns into **silage**. (Silage is rather like the rotted grass cuttings that you find in a compost heap.)

2.8 A field of wheat

Apart from the cattle and the fodder crops, Mr Dowding grows wheat (Photo 2.8), potatoes and swedes. The potatoes and swedes are packaged and sent to supermarkets.

2.7 Cutting grass to make silage

3 Read the section on mixed farming.

a Why are the cattle brought into the farmyard in the winter?

b How can grass be used to feed the cows in both summer and winter?

c Apart from grass, what else is grown on Aviaries Farm?

4 In 1997, Mr Dowding used his land as shown in Table 2.9.

a Present this information in the form of a bar graph or pie chart. Use different colours for each land use.

b Write a few sentences to describe how Mr Dowding used his land in 1997.

5 Study Figure 2.10. Organise the information into inputs, processes and outputs and present it using a diagram similar to Figure 1.2, page 39.

▼ *2.9*

Land use	No. of hectares
Grass (for grazing and silage)	206
Wheat	117
Potatoes	17
Fodder beet	12
Swedes	11
Kale and turnips (for cows to eat)	12
Vegetables	2
Other (e.g. woodland)	29
Total	**406**

▲ *2.10 Aviaries Farm – a jigsaw of inputs, processes and outputs*

A farmer's work is never done ...

There are a great many jobs to be done on Mr Dowding's farm throughout the year. Crops are sown, weeded and harvested. Land is ploughed, grass is cut for hay and silage. The cows are milked twice a day and there is always maintenance work, such as mending fences or repairing machines.

Look at the calendar in Figure 2.11 to find out some of the jobs Mr Dowding has to do from month to month.

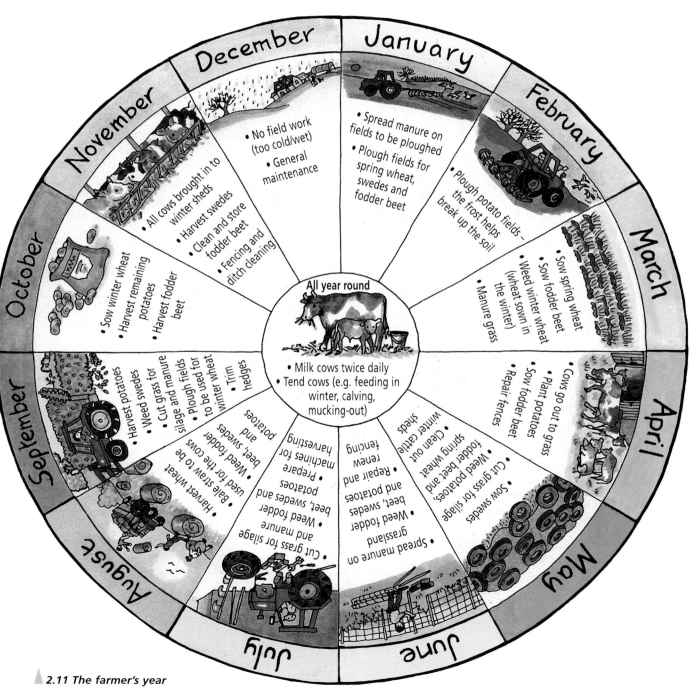

2.11 The farmer's year

6 Present the information in Figure 2.11, page 45, in the form of a table. Follow the steps below:

a Make a large copy of Table 2.12 on a sheet of graph paper.

b Choose colours for each of the activities listed in the key.

c Use your key to colour in the correct squares on your diagram. For example, use the 'plough' colour to shade in the February square for potatoes.

d Carefully write the maintenance jobs in their correct places.

7 Re-read the information in this unit and use the table you did for Activity 6, to answer the following questions.

a In which month are swedes sown?

b In which month are potatoes planted?

c When is grass cut for silage?

d What is silage used for?

e What happens to fodder beet after it has been harvested?

f When are all the cows brought in from the fields for the winter?

g What is the main maintenance job in July?

h Which months are the busiest?

i Which of the following farming activities is the most common:
- ploughing
- sowing
- weeding
- harvesting?

j How does the fact that Aviaries Farm is organic help to explain your answer to the last question?

	JAN	FEB	MAR	APR	MAY	JUN	JUL	AUG	SEPT	OCT	NOV	DEC
Food crops Winter wheat												
Spring wheat												
Potatoes												
Swedes												
Fodder crops Fodder beet											Clean and store	
Grass (silage)												
Cows				Out to grass		Milking	twice	daily			Winter sheds	
Maintenance												

Key

☐ Ploughing ☐ Harvesting and grass cutting

☐ Sowing/planting ☐ Manuring grass

☐ Weeding

2.12 The farmer's year, Aviaries Farm

welcome to
www.nfu.org.uk

nfu homepage

education

NFU Education Service : WORKING FARM STUDIES

Presenting profiles of 9 very different farms, drawn from each of the NFU regions
Sy'n cyflwyno 9 proffil o ffermydd gwahanol iawn, wedi'u dethol o bob un o ranbarthau Undeb Cenedlaethol yr Amaethwyr.

- Mixed farming and visitor centre - Central region
- Fferm gymysg a chanolfan ymwelwyr - rhanbarth Canolbarth Lloegr

- Arable - East Anglia region
- Fferm Tir Âr - rhanbarth East Anglia

- Horticulture with glasshouses - East Midlands region
- Garddwriaethol gyda thai gwydr - rhanbarth Dwyrain Canolbarth Lloegr

- Pigs - North East region
- Moch - rhanbarth Gogledd Dwyrain Lloegr

- Hill sheep - North West region
- Defaid Mynydd - rhanbarth Gogledd Orllewin Lloegr

- Soft fruit and hops - South East region
- Ffrwythau Meddal a Hopys - rhanbarth De Ddwyrain Lloegr

► - Organic dairy and arable - South West region
- Fferm laeth a thir âr organig - rhanbarth De Orllewin Lloegr

- Lowland beef - West Midlands region
- Iseldir - cig eidion - rhanbarth Gorllewin Canolbarth Lloegr

- Hill beef and sheep - Wales region
- Cig eidion a defaid mynydd - rhanbarth Cymru

- Glossary of farming terms

Email: **NFU@nfu.org.uk** Tel: 0171 331 7200 Fax : 0171 331 7313
Address: NFU, 164 Shaftesbury Avenue, London WC2H 8HL
Edit Site

▲ **2.13 The National Farmers' Union**

Web search

Aviaries Farm is one of 9 farm studies that can be found on the National Farmers' Union website at www.nfu.org.uk. Click 'education' and then 'farm studies' to obtain the menu page above (See Figure 2.13). Aviaries farm is the 'Organic, dairy and arable farm', which has been marked with an arrow. ►

- Find out more about the activities on Aviaries farm.
- Look at the map extract.
- Discover the most up-to-date figures regarding inputs, processes and outputs – how have they changed?
- What is the current role of the European Union?
- Use the 'hot links' to enter the 'glossary of farming terms'.

Compare the activities of Aviaries Farm with a contrasting farm in the UK.

3 Types of farming in Europe

Look at the main types of farming in Europe shown on Figure 3.1. Find the location of Aviaries Farm in the UK. Notice that it is located in an area of dairying. We already know that Mr Dowding keeps a lot of dairy cattle, however, he also grows crops such as wheat.

A map like Figure 3.1 gives a very generalised picture of farming types. Whilst one type of farming may dominate within each coloured area, farmers may also grow other crops or rear animals.

There is a great range of farming types in Europe. Perhaps the main cause of this is the variation in climate. The different climates of Europe mean, for example, that southern Europe is able to grow Mediterranean-type crops, whereas the wetter, cooler, western side of Europe is ideal for dairying and sheep farming. In some parts, such as northern Scandinavia, the climate is so cold that farming is very limited.

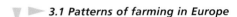
3.1 Patterns of farming in Europe

Mediterranean farming
Here conditions are ideal for crops such as citrus fruit (e.g. oranges and lemons), grapes, tomatoes and olives. They thrive in the hot, sunny conditions and can cope with low rainfall.

Dairying
The high rainfall, brought in off the Atlantic Ocean by the prevailing westerly winds, encourages the growth of lush, good-quality grass in these areas. In addition, the mild winters mean that the cattle can graze outside throughout the year. (They only need to be brought under cover during particularly cold spells.)

Mixed farming
This type of farming is most widespread in Europe. It involves growing crops, such as wheat and potatoes, and rearing animals like pigs and cattle. These areas have a moderate climate with few extremes of temperature or rainfall.

Sheep
Sheep can survive in harsh weather conditions. They are well suited to mountain areas and can live on poor-quality mountain grass. Flocks often roam freely over vast areas of rough moorland. They are only rounded up by farmers for shearing, medical treatment or when they are lambing.

Cereals
Cereal crops include wheat, barley and oats. Cereals grow best in areas that are fairly dry and, where the summers are warm and sunny to help the crops ripen. Cereals are grown in huge, flat fields. Farmers are able to use large machinery in these fields. They harvest large quantities very efficiently.

Reindeer

Reindeer are very hardy and can survive the intense cold of north European winters. They graze grassland and forest floors and provide meat and skins for the Sami people who rear them. They are also sold to buy food and other items (see page 113 for further details).

Unsuitable for farming

These areas are either too steep and mountainous, such as parts of the Alps, or too cold and inhospitable for farming. In Scandinavia, much of the land is used for forestry as trees are well suited to the climate. In Iceland, much of the land is mountainous, rocky or covered by glaciers.

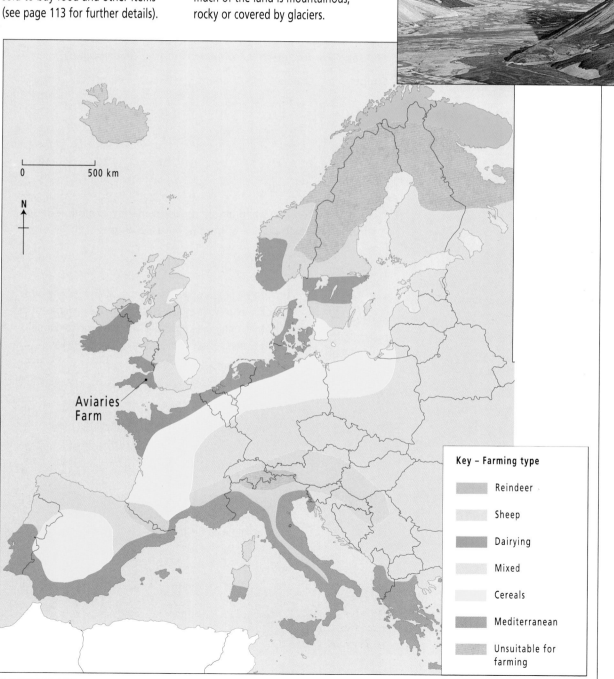

0   500 km

N

Aviaries Farm

Key – Farming type

Reindeer

Sheep

Dairying

Mixed

Cereals

Mediterranean

Unsuitable for farming

1 You will need an outline map of Europe for this activity.

a Using Figure 3.1, plot the distribution of farming types onto your map. Use a pencil first and then colours.

b Name the areas that are 'unsuitable for farming'. Look at Atlas Map B, page 11, if you need help.

c Label the European Union countries. (You may need to refer to Figure 1.2, page 5.)

2 You may decide to do this activity in rough first, and then copy it out neatly.

a Make a large copy of Table 3.2.

b Complete the table using Figure 3.1 and Atlas Maps A and B, pages 10–11. For details about Europe's climate, turn to Figure 2.2, page 15.

▼ **3.2 Summary of farming types in Europe**

Type of farming	Description of farming	Climate characteristics	Areas of Europe
Reindeer			
Sheep			
Dairying			
Mixed			
Cereals			
Mediterranean			

▼ **3.3 Land use for selected European countries (percentages)**

Country	Arable*	Permanent	Grass	Forestry	Other crops**
UK	27	0	46	10	17
Italy	31	10	17	23	19
Sweden	7	0	1	68	24
Austria	17	1	24	39	19
Denmark	60	0	5	10	25

* crops grown on ploughed land e.g. wheat, barley and oilseed rape
* * bushes and tree crops e.g. grapes, olives, oranges

3 Study the photos in Figure 3.1.

a Photos A and B show two types of farming. For each one, describe the scene in as much detail as you can. What is happening? What is the land like? What type of farming is taking place?

b Now look at Photo C. Why do you think the area shown is unsuitable for farming?

4 Table 3.3 contains data about land use. This information can be presented in the form of a diagram called a **proportional bar**. Figure 3.4 is an example of one.

a Look carefully at Table 3.3 and Figure 3.4. Which country's data is shown in the proportional bar in Figure 3.4?

b Draw a proportional bar for the UK and for one other country of your choice. Place them one underneath the other, using the same scale. Use the same colour on both bars for each land use, e.g. arable = yellow.

c Give your diagram a title and a key.

d Write a couple of sentences describing the differences between your two bars.

e Try to suggest some reasons for the differences.

f Can you suggest some land uses that might form the 'other' percentages?

5 Climate is one of the most important factors affecting farming types. Write a few sentences about the effect of climate on the pattern of farming in Europe.

▼ **3.4**

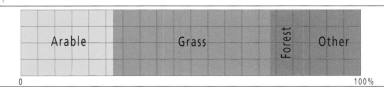

4 Leisure Farms: farms of the future?

Some farmers in the UK have decided to earn extra money by opening their farms to the public. Families are invited to touch and feed the animals, fields are turned into go-kart tracks and ponds become fishing lakes. Farm shops offer fruit and vegetables, bread and jams, and children's toys such as tractors and farm animals. This is called **farm diversification**.

Look at Figure 4.1, pages 52–53. It is a plan of Trethorne Leisure Farm, located near Launceston in Cornwall. It used to be a dairy farm but in 1987 the farmers, Mr and Mrs Davey, decided to diversify and open it to the public. Over the years, the Leisure Farm expanded to take up the whole farm. There is even an 18-hole golf course now. In 1998, over 50 000 people visited the farm to enjoy the huge range of activities on offer.

1 Read the information on leisure farms.

a What is meant by the term 'farm diversification'?

b Why have some farmers decided to diversify?

Bottle feed the Lambs

Falconry displays on Monday to Friday (weather permitting)

Milk Daisy, our cow, by hand

OPEN ALL YEAR (Mon–Sat)

40,000 sq ft UNDERCOVER

Trethorne Leisure Farm

AND GOLF COURSE
Nr. Launceston, Cornwall

ALL WEATHER ENTERTAINMENT

ANIMALS TO HOLD, FEED, MILK & CUDDLE
FREE HORSE & PONY RIDES

EXCITING NEW VENTURE OPENING

Supported by
The English Tourist Board
ALL INCLUSIVE ENTRANCE FEE NO HIDDEN EXTRAS

TRETHORNE LEISURE FOR PLEASURE

2 Study Figure 4.1.

a Where are falconry displays held (give the reference number on the map) and on what days of the week?

b You have arranged to meet a friend for a game of crazy golf. Describe where the crazy golf area is located.

c In pairs, look carefully at the activities and places to visit at Trethorne Leisure Farm.

- Find three places or activities that would appeal to an adult visitor.
- Find six places that a toddler would enjoy visiting.
- What would you choose to do if you visited the farm? Give reasons for your answer.

d What evidence is there that this farm used to be a dairy farm?

4.1 Plan of Trethorne Leisure Farm, Cornwall

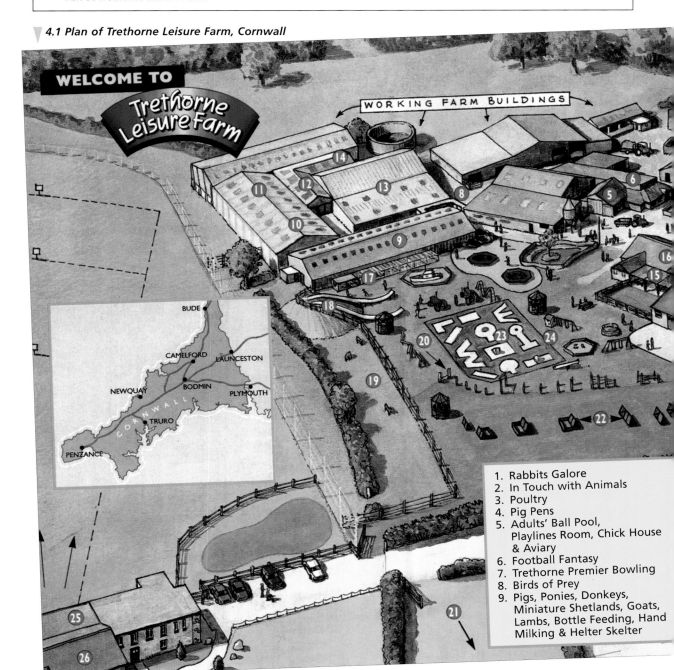

1. Rabbits Galore
2. In Touch with Animals
3. Poultry
4. Pig Pens
5. Adults' Ball Pool, Playlines Room, Chick House & Aviary
6. Football Fantasy
7. Trethorne Premier Bowling
8. Birds of Prey
9. Pigs, Ponies, Donkeys, Miniature Shetlands, Goats, Lambs, Bottle Feeding, Hand Milking & Helter Skelter

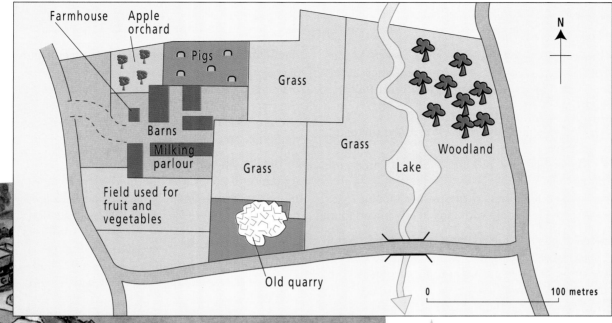

The map labels: Farmhouse, Apple orchard, Pigs, Grass, Woodland, N, Barns, Milking parlour, Grass, Grass, Lake, Field used for fruit and vegetables, Old quarry, 0 100 metres

▲ **4.2 Plan of Cherry Tree Farm**

9TH GREEN

10. Rabbits, Deer, Cattle, Lambs, Pirate Adventure, Mother & Baby Room
11. Gladiator Duel, 3-Tier Maze, Skittles, Sand Pit & Baby Calves (*January – April*)
12. Trampoline Room, Astra Slide, Free-fall Slide and Shop
13. Country Capers Play Area, Indoor Assault Course, Toddler Play Area
14. Toilets
15. Toilets
16. Restaurants & Inside Toilets
17. Peacock & Guinea Fowl Aviaries
18. 30 Foot Family Slides
19. Deer Enclosure
20. Adult Trim Trail (*Mums & Dads lose a bit of weight*)
21. Falconry Displays Mon-Fri (*weather permitting*)
22. Rare Breeds of Poultry
23. Crazy Golf
24. Childrens' Play Area & Family Picnic Park
25. Golf Driving Range
26. Golf Clubhouse
27. Farmhouse Accommodation

3 Look at Figure 4.2. Cherry Tree Farm is a working dairy farm but the farmer wants to diversify in order to earn more money.

a Look carefully at the layout of Cherry Tree Farm and make a list of some of the activities and enterprises that the farmer could introduce. Use Figure 4.1 to help you, along with any information about similar farms near to you.

b On a copy of Figure 4.2, show what you would do to change the farm. Locate your activities and enterprises using colours and a key. Try not to do too much as it is a small farm.

c Write a few sentences, giving reasons for the changes you have suggested.

d Design a single-sided advert for the farm, to appear in a local newspaper.

5 The Common Agricultural Policy

The European Union effects many aspects of our everyday lives. Farmers in particular are greatly influenced by the **Common Agricultural Policy (CAP)**.

The CAP was introduced in 1962. It had three main aims:
- To increase food production in the European Union
- To provide farmers with a secure income
- To provide people with reasonably priced food.

The CAP has had mixed success. Food production has increased, although, for a time, there was over-production resulting in **food surpluses**. The unwanted food cost an enormous amount to store. In addition, there have been some damaging effects on the environment (see Figure 5.1). Farmers have had a fairly secure income, although some would say that their incomes have not risen very much. Whilst the price of food has risen, it probably hasn't risen as much as if there had been no CAP.

In 1984 and again in 1992, the Common Agricultural Policy was reformed to try to make it more successful. Some of the new policies are described in Figure 5.2. Since 1992, production has dropped and there are fewer food surpluses. Farming has become more environmentally-friendly, with fewer chemicals being used, and farmers being encouraged to plant hedges and woodlands.

Hedgerows are valuable habitats to a great variety of wildlife. They are being cut down as fields are enlarged to increase production. This has led to a rapid loss of topsoil due to wind erosion in some areas.

ENVIRONMENTAL PROBLEMS RESULTING FROM THE COMMON AGRICULTURAL POLICY

Chemicals used in pesticides and fertilisers harm animals and birds... and can seep into underground water and pollute it.

UNDERGROUND WATER

Wetland – home to many rare species...

Wetland habitats are being drained to turn more land into farm land.

5.1

Aviaries Farm and the CAP

Mr Dowding, the owner of Aviaries Farm in Unit 2 of this chapter, has been greatly affected by the CAP. Whilst there is a big market for milk produced on organic farms, the CAP **milk quota** prevents Mr Dowding producing as much milk as he could sell. Mr Dowding does, however, receive a guaranteed price for his wheat and some of his land has been taken out of production as **land set-aside** (see Figure 5.2). He also receives grants for tree and hedge planting and for repairing dry-stone walls.

1 Read the information on CAP.

a What do the letters CAP stand for?

b What were the original aims of the CAP?

2 Study Figure 5.1. With the aid of simple sketches, describe some of the environmental problems that have been linked with increasing agricultural production.

3 Study Figure 5.2.

a What are milk quotas and why were they introduced?

b Why is Mr Dowding not happy about milk quotas?

c In what ways does Mr Dowding benefit from the CAP?

5.2

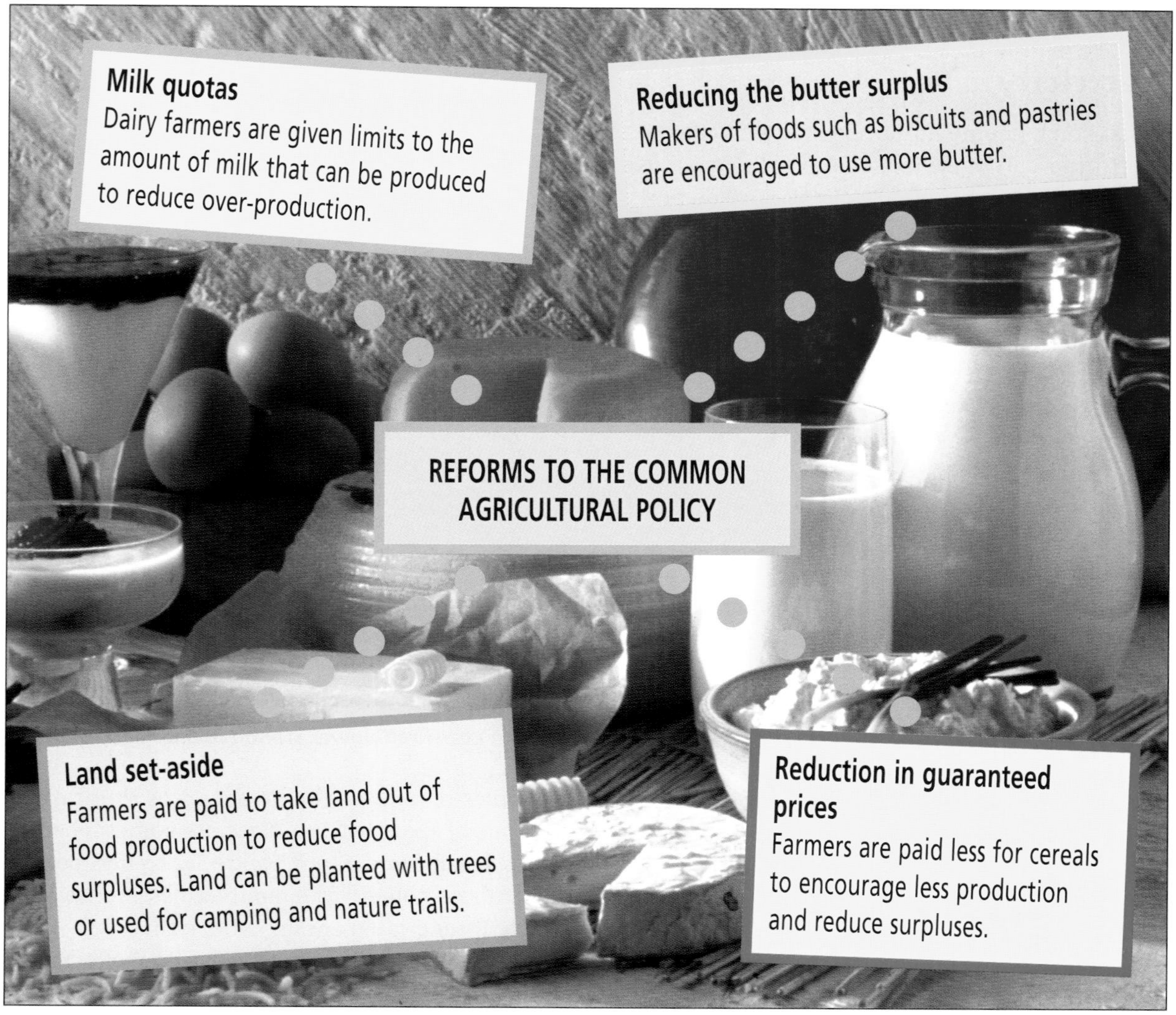

Milk quotas
Dairy farmers are given limits to the amount of milk that can be produced to reduce over-production.

Reducing the butter surplus
Makers of foods such as biscuits and pastries are encouraged to use more butter.

REFORMS TO THE COMMON AGRICULTURAL POLICY

Land set-aside
Farmers are paid to take land out of food production to reduce food surpluses. Land can be planted with trees or used for camping and nature trails.

Reduction in guaranteed prices
Farmers are paid less for cereals to encourage less production and reduce surpluses.

Energy

Energy is the power that we use to keep us warm, cook our food, drive our machines and run most of the equipment that is part of our daily lives. Much of our energy comes in the form of electricity which is produced in power stations.

1 Types of energy

Electricity

Whilst some people in Europe still get heat direct from burning wood, peat or coal, most use energy in the form of **electricity**. It is clean and simple to use in the home – most power for cooking, heating, lighting and running appliances such as fridges, microwaves and televisions comes from electricity.

Electricity is produced at **power stations** like the one in Photo 1.1. At Saarland in Germany, coal from nearby mines is burned to generate electricity, which is then sent down power lines to industry and homes. Other power stations generate electricity by burning gas, oil and even waste products such as paper and straw. Electricity can also be generated by nuclear power and by using the power of the elements such as water, wind and the sun.

▲ *1.1 A coal-fired power station in Saarland, Germany*

Burning away our future …

You may have heard of the terms **renewable** and **non-renewable**. A renewable source of energy does not run out or get used up. Examples of renewable sources are moving water (rivers, tides and waves), the wind and the sun. Non-renewable sources do get used up and will eventually run out. Coal, oil and gas are good examples of non-renewable energy as they take millions of years to form. They are sometimes called **fossil fuels**. Study Figure 1.2 to find out more about some of the main forms of renewable and non-renewable energy. Notice that generating electricity can have harmful effects on the environment.

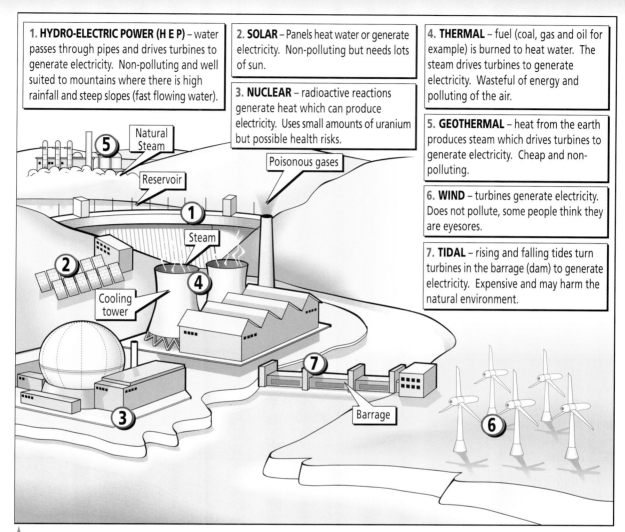

1. **HYDRO-ELECTRIC POWER (H E P)** – water passes through pipes and drives turbines to generate electricity. Non-polluting and well suited to mountains where there is high rainfall and steep slopes (fast flowing water).

2. **SOLAR** – Panels heat water or generate electricity. Non-polluting but needs lots of sun.

3. **NUCLEAR** – radioactive reactions generate heat which can produce electricity. Uses small amounts of uranium but possible health risks.

4. **THERMAL** – fuel (coal, gas and oil for example) is burned to heat water. The steam drives turbines to generate electricity. Wasteful of energy and polluting of the air.

5. **GEOTHERMAL** – heat from the earth produces steam which drives turbines to generate electricity. Cheap and non-polluting.

6. **WIND** – turbines generate electricity. Does not pollute, some people think they are eyesores.

7. **TIDAL** – rising and falling tides turn turbines in the barrage (dam) to generate electricity. Expensive and may harm the natural environment.

Natural Steam · Reservoir · Poisonous gases · Steam · Cooling tower · Barrage

▲ *1.2 Ways of generating electricity*

1 Energy is used to power trains and cars, run computers and boil kettles. Make a list, or produce a collage, using simple sketches to show how important energy is in our daily lives.

2 What is the difference between renewable and non-renewable energy?

3 Study Figure 1.2.

a Which types of electricity generation are renewable?

b Describe how light from the sun can be turned into electricity.

c Give two reasons why hydro-electric power is well suited to mountain areas.

d How is electricity generated in a thermal power station like the one shown in Photo 1.1?

e What type of energy generation uses heat from the earth?

f Describe how some forms of electricity generation might be harmful to the environment.

4 Choose one type of renewable energy generation shown on Figure 1.2. Write a few sentences about your chosen example and include a simple sketch from Figure 1.2. Use reference books or CD-ROMs to find out more about your chosen type.

2 Non-renewable energy: oil

One of the most important sources of energy today is oil. Oil provides fuel for transport. It is burned in power stations to generate electricity. In addition, it provides raw materials for a variety of industries. Figure 2.1 shows the variety of uses that we have for oil.

How is it formed?

Like coal, oil is a good example of a non-renewable fossil fuel. It was formed millions of years ago from microscopic **plankton** that lived in the sea. When they died they sunk to the sea bed. Slowly chemical changes turned the plankton into black, treacle-like **crude oil** (see Figure 2.2). Notice that natural gas was also formed in much the same way.

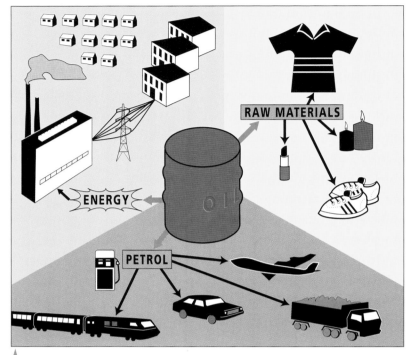

2.1 Uses of oil

2.2 How crude oil forms

1 Millions of years ago, dead microscopic plants and animals called **plankton**, collected on the sea bed.

Plankton under a microscope

2 Plankton and deposited muds are slowly buried by other sediment. Chemical changes at high temperatures turn the plankton into **crude oil**. The sediments slowly turn into rock.

Plankton-rich rock

3 Earth movements fold the rocks. Crude oil collects in **anticlines** (upfolds) of porous rock such as sandstone. The pores (holes) in the sandstone help to store the oil – this layer of rock is called a **reservoir rock**. Geologists searching for oil look out for these upfolds – they call them **oil traps**.

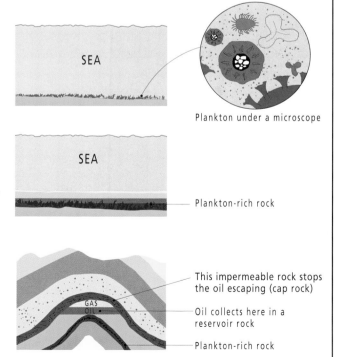

This impermeable rock stops the oil escaping (cap rock)

Oil collects here in a reservoir rock

Plankton-rich rock

North Sea oil and gas

The North Sea is one of the richest areas of oil and gas in the world. Exploration began in the 1960s and the first oilfield, the Ekofisk field, was discovered in 1969. During the 1970s, more and more oil was found and brought ashore.

Look at Figure 2.3. Notice that the North Sea has been split up between the various countries that border it. Each of the areas is called a **sector**. Which two countries have the largest sectors? Why do you think this is?

Although the oil and gas may belong to a particular country, the drilling and much of the refining is done by huge companies such as Shell, BP and Esso. These massive companies operate all over the world. They are called **multinationals**. Multinationals spend vast amounts of money on looking for, extracting, and processing oil and gas.

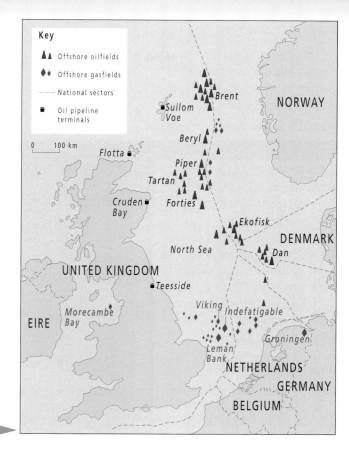

2.3 Oil and gas fields

1 Study Figure 2.2 .

a From what organisms did oil form?

b What happened to turn the dead organisms into crude oil?

c What is an anticline?

d Why does an anticline form an oil trap?

e What name is given to the impermeable rock that stops the oil escaping?

f Why do you think the rock that contains the oil is called a reservoir rock?

g Why is oil a non-renewable fossil fuel?

2 Study Figure 2.3.

a Which country owns the Forties oilfield?

b Which country owns the Ekofisk oilfield?

c In which country is the greatest number of gasfields?

e Copy and complete the following sentence using the correct word in the brackets.

Most of the gasfields are in the (northern/southern) North Sea and most of the oilfields are in the (southern/northern) North Sea.

f Which pipeline terminal do you think the Forties field sends its oil to?

3 Look at Table 2.4.

a On graph paper, draw a bar chart to illustrate the figures.

b Do you notice anything interesting about your chart?

c Give your chart a title.

2.4 Oil production (million tonnes) 1996

UK	130
Norway	156
Denmark	10
Netherlands	2.3
Germany	3.1

Life on an oil rig

Oil and gas is extracted from the rocks beneath the North Sea by huge oil rigs that are floated out to sea. The oil and gas is transported to refineries on land by pipelines lying on the sea bed. Working on an oil rig involves hard work and very long hours as Figure 2. 5 describes.
Helicopters are vital for carrying the workers to and from the rigs.

▼ *2.5 Life on the Tartan oil platform*

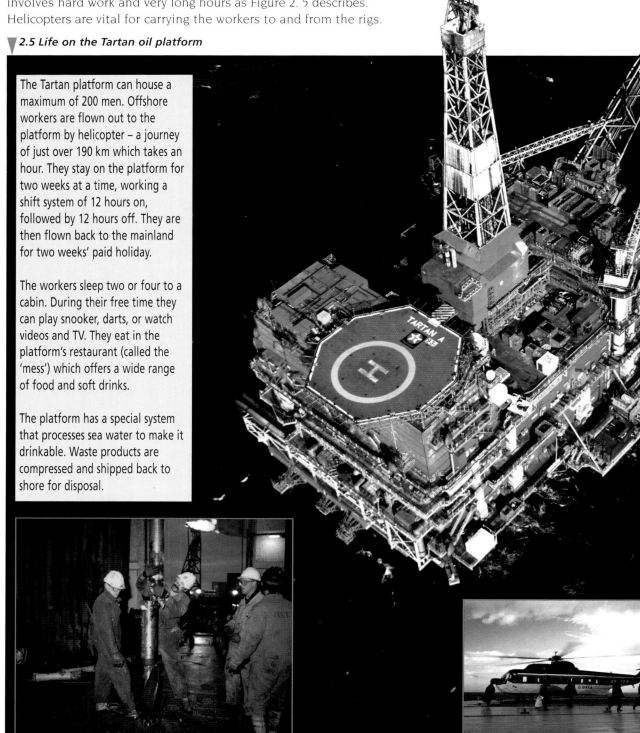

The Tartan platform can house a maximum of 200 men. Offshore workers are flown out to the platform by helicopter – a journey of just over 190 km which takes an hour. They stay on the platform for two weeks at a time, working a shift system of 12 hours on, followed by 12 hours off. They are then flown back to the mainland for two weeks' paid holiday.

The workers sleep two or four to a cabin. During their free time they can play snooker, darts, or watch videos and TV. They eat in the platform's restaurant (called the 'mess') which offers a wide range of food and soft drinks.

The platform has a special system that processes sea water to make it drinkable. Waste products are compressed and shipped back to shore for disposal.

What price oil?

The North Sea, with its violent storms and thick fogs, is one of the most dangerous drilling environments in the world. Occasionally accidents happen – helicopters crash and men are killed or injured from working in the extreme conditions. In 1988, the world's worst oil platform disaster occurred when an explosion ripped through the Piper Alpha oil platform in the North Sea, killing 167 men. In 1996, an oil tanker, the *Sea Empress*, ran aground off Milford Haven in South Wales. Over 200 km of coastline was affected by oil pollution and thousands of sea birds died.

In 1995 there was an uproar when Shell planned to dispose of an old oil platform, the Brent Spar, by sinking it in the North Sea – many people were worried that the platform would pollute the sea. They also thought that other companies would do the same thing, and before long, the sea bed would be littered with old platforms.

▲ *2.6 Brent Spar being towed into harbour*

The platform has 13 gas turbines, similar to those used to power jet engines, which generate heat and light – enough to power a small town. It also has its own mini-hospital. However, most cases involving serious injury or illness are sent ashore by helicopter.

Deliveries of letters, parcels and newspapers are made at least three times a week by helicopter. If it is too foggy or stormy to fly, a supply vessel will be used. Supply vessels normally visit Tartan twice a week, carrying everything from ice cream and toothpaste, to heavy tools and equipment for the rig.

There are telephone links, telex facilities and weather facsimile systems which provide printed weather charts.

Everybody undergoes strict safety training. Special protective clothing, including safety helmets, gloves, boots and fluorescent waterproof overalls, must be worn at all times when working.

4 Study the information in Figure 2.5.

a How long do oil workers stay out on the platform?

b What can the workers do in their time off?

c Describe what you think it must be like to work on a remote oil platform. What would you miss from home? Write a postcard home to your family describing what life is like.

5 Study the section and write a few sentences to describe how oil can pollute the environment.

(Teachers might like to support Activity 5 with GeoActive 174 Autumn 1997)

3 Renewable energy: wind

The power of the wind has been harnessed by people for centuries. At sea, people use wind to power sailing boats and ships. On land, in parts of Europe, windmills still grind wheat to make flour and pump water to drain or irrigate land for farming.

Large turbines are used to generate electricity from wind. Clusters of turbines are called **wind farms** (see photo 3.1). Each turbine consists of a two- or three-bladed propellor mounted on a 30–60 metre pole. As the wind blows, the propellor spins round and generates electricity.

Advantages and disadvantages of wind power

Wind is freely available and it does not run out, although it can stop for a while. It is, therefore, a good example of a renewable form of energy. Generating electricity using wind does not produce harmful gases that might damage the environment. Some people feel that wind turbines are elegant structures, just as windmills are, and that they will be very useful to us in the future.

There are, however, some disadvantages. The turbines are expensive and only operate when the wind is over five metres per second. Other people consider the turbines to be ugly. They think that they spoil the countryside. Wind farms can be noisy, although recent ones are much quieter than they used to be.

Wind energy in Europe

Wind could be one of the most important forms of renewable energy in the future. Figure 3.2 shows relative wind speeds in Europe. The highest wind speeds are found in northern Europe due to the strong winds that blow off the Atlantic Ocean.

There are some other isolated pockets of high wind speeds, for example, in southern France and to the south of the Pyrenees. These areas are affected by strong local winds. One of these is the Mistral which blows along the lower Rhône valley in France.

▲ *3.1 A wind farm*

1 Look at Photo 3.1.
a Make a sketch of one of the wind turbines in the photo.
b Label the propellor.
c Draw a vertical line alongside to show that its height from the ground is 60 metres.
d Use the scale line that you have drawn to show roughly how tall you would be if you stood next to the turbine.

2 Take some time to look closely at Photo 3.1. Write a couple of sentences about the effect of the turbines on the landscape. Do you think they are elegant structures or an eyesore?

Much of Europe has strong enough winds to be able to generate electricity. Germany and Denmark have already spent a lot of money on producing wind energy. In the UK, we have 34 wind farms (Figure 3.3) that produce about 1 per cent of our electricity. In Denmark, wind energy accounts for about 5 per cent of all electricity generated. Turbines have even been constructed out to sea (see Photo 3.4, page 64).

3.2 Wind map of Europe ▶

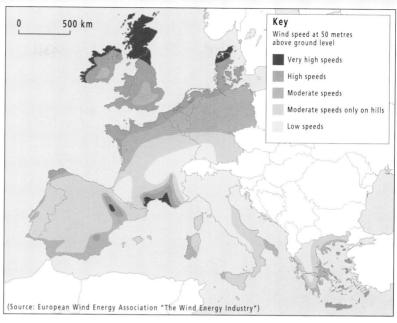

Key
Wind speed at 50 metres above ground level

Very high speeds
High speeds
Moderate speeds
Moderate speeds only on hills
Low speeds

(Source: European Wind Energy Association "The Wind Energy Industry")

▼ **3.3 UK wind farms**

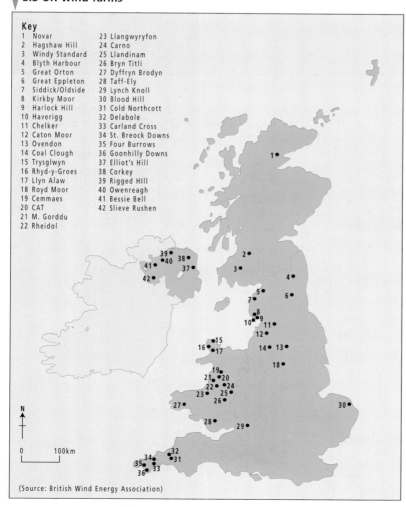

Key
1 Novar
2 Hagshaw Hill
3 Windy Standard
4 Blyth Harbour
5 Great Orton
6 Great Eppleton
7 Siddick/Oldside
8 Kirkby Moor
9 Harlock Hill
10 Haverigg
11 Chelker
12 Caton Moor
13 Ovendon
14 Coal Clough
15 Trysglwyn
16 Rhyd-y-Groes
17 Llyn Alaw
18 Royd Moor
19 Cemmaes
20 CAT
21 M. Gorddu
22 Rheidol
23 Llangwyryfon
24 Carno
25 Llandinam
26 Bryn Titli
27 Dyffryn Brodyn
28 Taff-Ely
29 Lynch Knoll
30 Blood Hill
31 Cold Northcott
32 Delabole
33 Carland Cross
34 St. Breock Downs
35 Four Burrows
36 Goonhilly Downs
37 Elliot's Hill
38 Corkey
39 Rigged Hill
40 Owenreagh
41 Bessie Bell
42 Slieve Rushen

(Source: British Wind Energy Association)

3 For this activity you will need an outline map of the UK. You are going to draw a map: 'Wind speeds and the location of wind farms in the UK'.

a Use Figure 3.2 to help you plot the UK wind speeds on your map. You can use the same colours as Figure 3.2 or choose your own, but make sure that the darkest colour shows the highest wind speeds.

b Now, on the same map, plot the locations of the UK wind farms, shown on Figure 3.3. (You do not have to label each one.)

c Describe the location of the wind farms in the UK. Consider if they are mostly in the east or the west, the north or the south? Are they inland or quite close to the sea? Does there appear to be any pattern?

d Are there any parts of the UK which have high wind speeds, yet few wind farms?

▲ *3.4 Coastal wind farm in Denmark*

4 Look at Table 3.5.

a Plot this information in the form of a bar chart, using a different colour for each country.

b Which country makes most use of wind energy?

c Look at Figure 3.2. Would you expect the country, given as your answer to the last question, to obtain most of its wind energy from the north or the south? Explain your answer.

d Use Figure 3.2 to explain why wind energy is also relatively important in the UK and Denmark.

e Use Figure 3.2 to suggest which country, that currently produces very little wind energy, has the potential to produce quite a lot more. Where would you suggest wind turbines could be located? (Use Atlas Map B, page 11, to help you.)

▼ *3.5 Wind energy in selected European countries*

Country	Wind energy (megawatts)
Denmark	835
France	5.7
Germany	1552
Greece	29
Italy	70.5
Ireland	11
Netherlands	299
Portugal	19.1
Spain	249
Sweden	103
UK	273

Web search

Conduct a research project on wind energy in Denmark. There is a lot of excellent information available on the Internet at www.windpower. DK

4 Conserving energy

There are many ways that energy can be conserved in the home (see Figure 4.1). Houses can be **insulated** to keep the heat in. This can be done by having insulation in the attic and in-between the spaces in the walls. Governments can pass laws and encourage people in various ways to save energy.

1 Study Figure 4.1 , below.

a What is insulation and where should you find it in the home?

b How much longer do low energy light bulbs last compared with ordinary ones?

c How much money is wasted in a year if a hot water cylinder does not have a jacket on it?

▼ *4.1 Conserving energy in the home*

How can we conserve energy?

Demand for energy is growing very rapidly. With electricity so easily available, at the 'flick of a switch', many of us have become wasteful. Think how many times you leave lights on at home and how often your classroom is left empty but with the lights on.

As the demand for electricity increases, more and more fossil fuels are burned. You have probably heard of **global warming** and **acid rain**. These are two environmental problems that are caused in part by the burning of fossil fuels to produce electricity.

One solution is to switch to renewable forms of energy but these tend to be very expensive. An alternative solution involves reducing our demand for energy. This is called **energy conservation**.

Power stations that produce electricity waste a lot of energy. Some of this is in the form of hot water. In a few countries, this hot water is used to heat houses, offices and factories. This is called **combined heat and power**, or CHP. In Denmark many houses are supplied with hot water in this way and it reduces the use of energy by about 30 per cent.

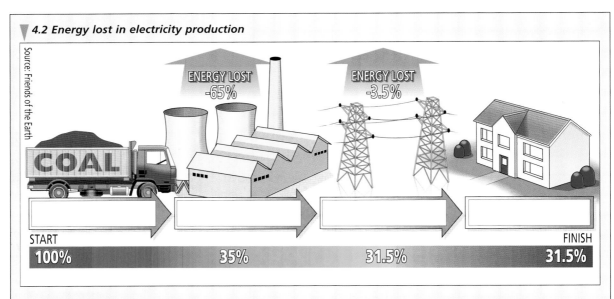

▼ **4.2 Energy lost in electricity production**

Source: Friends of the Earth

ENERGY LOST -65%

ENERGY LOST -3.5%

COAL

START 100% 35% 31.5% FINISH 31.5%

2 Make a copy of Figure 4.2.

a Write each of the following labels next to the correct arrow:
- Power lines ● Home ● Raw coal ● Power station.

b At what stage in the generation of electricity is most energy lost?

c What percentage of energy is lost in total?

d What is combined heat and power (CHP)?

e How does Figure 4.2 support the case for CHP?

3 Study Table 4. 3.

a Draw a pie chart to show how electricity is used in the home. Write the percentage used in or above each section.

b Can you suggest some uses of electricity that would belong in the 'Others' category?

▼ **4.3 How electricity is used in the home (%)**

Room heating	21
Fridge/freezer	18
Hot water	12
Lighting	10
Cooking	8
Washing	8
TV	5
Other	18

4 Carry out a survey of energy use and conservation in your home.

a Copy out questions 1 – 6 from Figure 4.4 and answer them at home. Change any questions if they do not apply to your home e.g. if your home is not heated by radiators, replace question 3 with one that is relevant. (You may have to ask an adult to help you answer some of the questions.)

b When you have finished, discuss your findings with your family and then fill in the 'Conclusions' section. You can write down as many points as you wish. Remember that everyone can save energy in their own small way – switching off lights and, having showers rather than baths, are both energy-saving measures.

c Finally, design a poster to display at home called: 'Action plan for conserving energy at home'. (It can be illustrated with cartoons if you wish.) Include ideas for the future such as buying energy-efficient appliances, as well as smaller ones that you can do every day. (Use Figure 4.1 as a guide.)

d Compare your survey's findings with others in the class.

5 In groups, carry out a survey of energy use and conservation in your school. Follow similar steps to those in Activity 4 and display your work in the form of a poster.

▼ *4.4 Survey*

Energy conservation in the home

1 Do you have insulation   YES   NO
    – in the attic/loft ☐ ☐
    – in the outside wall (cavity insulation)? ☐ ☐

2 Are the windows double-glazed? ☐ ☐

3 Do the radiators have individual thermostats to control temperature? ☐ ☐

4 Is the hot water tank lagged? ☐ ☐

5 Have you recently bought an appliance e.g. a fridge or washing machine? ☐ ☐
    If yes, is it a low energy one? ☐ ☐

6 Do you have low energy light bulbs? ☐ ☐
    If yes, how many do you have?
    1   2–5   6+
    ☐   ☐   ☐

Don't copy or fill in 7 and 8 until you have answered questions 1–6 and discussed your findings at home

Conclusions
7 We waste energy in the following ways:
1 _____
2 _____
3 _____

You can write down lots more points here

8 How can we conserve energy?
   Every day:
1 _____
2 _____
3 _____

Write down more points if you want

   In the future:
1 _____
2 _____
3 _____
4 _____

Again, add more points if you want

Ice

Ice is one of the most powerful types of erosion. Vast glaciers (rivers of ice), over 1 km in depth, have carved huge valleys and created dramatic mountain scenery in Europe. Many people enjoy walking and skiing in glacial areas but they have to be careful to avoid the hazard of avalanches.

1 Ice in the Alps

Look at Photo 1.2, which shows part of the Mont Blanc mountain range (find Mont Blanc on Atlas Map B, page 11). This landscape is being actively eroded by ice – you can see two glaciers in the photo. Above the glaciers are steep and jagged mountains. These are being actively weathered by **frost shattering**.

Let's now discover more about two of the features in Photo 1.2.

The Mer de Glace glacier

The main **glacier** on Photo 1.2 is called the Mer de Glace (what do you think this means in English?). The Mer de Glace is 7 km long, 1200 metres wide and up to 200 metres thick. Ice moves within the glacier at a speed of about 70 metres a year. Figure 1.1 shows the location of the Mer de Glace.

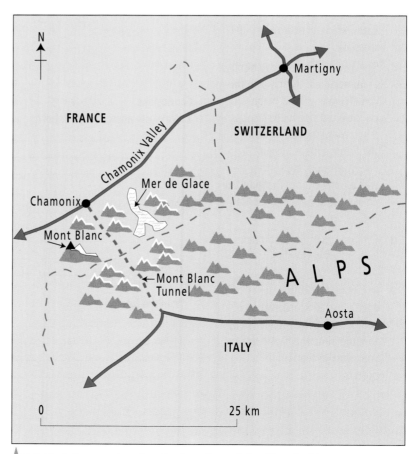

▲ *1.1 Sketch map showing the location of the Mer de Glace*

▲ *1.2 An aerial view of the Mer de Glace glacier in the Alps*

1 Study Photo 1.2.

a Write a few sentences or a poem, describing the scene to someone who cannot see the photo. Try to get across the dramatic nature of the landscape.

b Does the landscape appeal to you? Explain your answer.

2 The many sharp mountain peaks are known by the local French-speakers as 'aguilles'.

a Try to discover what this word means.

b Why do you think this word is used?

Look at the glacier in Photo 1.3. Notice that it is covered with rock fragments and boulders. This debris is called **moraine**. It comes mostly from the bare mountainsides above the glacier as a result of frost shattering.

Photo 1.4 is a close-up of the valley side, looking in the opposite direction, down the glacier. Notice the huge boulder and the smooth rock surface to the left. This surface was smoothed when the Mer de Glace was even bigger that it is today. As a glacier moves down a valley, boulders (like the one in the photo) scrape and gouge the valley sides, in the same way that sandpaper smooths a wood surface. This process is called **abrasion**. It is one of the most important ways that a glacier erodes a landscape.

1.3 Moraine on the Mer de Glace

3 Study Photo 1.3. Look at the rocks on the surface of the ice.

a Describe the rocks that are on the ice. Are they large or small, rounded or angular?

b What name is given to this debris lying on the ice?

c How did the rocks get onto the ice?

4 One of the main processes of erosion is abrasion.

a Describe in your own words how the process works.

b Now look at Photo 1.4. What are the effects of abrasion on the valley wall?

1.4 Evidence of abrasion at the edge of the Mer de Glace

Features of a glacier

Study Figure 1.5. You have already seen some of these features in the earlier photos.

A glacier is fed by new snow, mostly high up in the mountains, where it is coldest. Over many years the snow becomes compacted to form ice. It then starts to move downhill due to the force of gravity. The front of a glacier is called its **snout** (see Photo 1.6). Huge amounts of moraine build up at the snout and buries the ice. In the summer, it becomes warm at this lower altitude and some of the ice melts.

1.5 The snout of a glacier in the Italian Alps

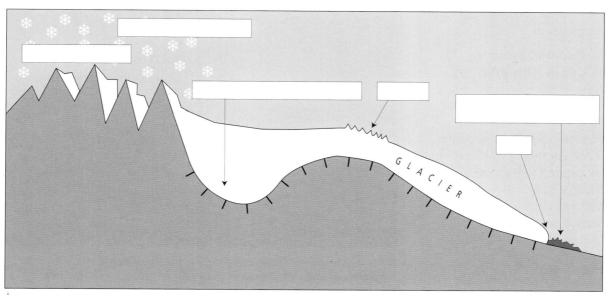

GLACIER

1.6 Typical features of a glacier

---

5 Make a copy of Figure 1.6.

a Complete the boxes by writing in the correct labels.
- cirque – deep bowl shaped landform
- snout
- jagged mountain peaks
- terminal moraine – a pile of moraine at the snout
- heavy snowfall in mountains
- crevasses

b Do you think most of the ice has formed near the top of the glacier or near the bottom? Explain your answer.

c Why do you think most melting occurs in the summer?

d Why do you think most melting takes place near the snout of a glacier?

6 Study Photo 1.5. Describe the shape and surface of the glacier snout.

Crevasses

Crevasses are cracks in the ice (see Photo 1.2). They are usually a few metres across and several metres deep. The deepest crevasses, found in Antarctica and Greenland, are over 30 metres deep but most are between 5 and 10 metres deep. Crevasses are formed when the ice is forced to stretch and then crack as it flows down a steep slope (see Figure 1.6, page 71).

Look at Photo 1.7. Notice the glacier looks blue inside. This colour is typical and is caused by the ice being extremely dense. The man in the photo gives you an idea of the size of the crevasse.

Crevasses are extremely dangerous. They open and close as the glacier moves. They are often hidden under fresh snow and skiers and walkers have to watch out for them. For this reason, it is very important to be properly equipped and have an expert with you when you venture onto a glacier.

1.7 A skier approaching a giant crevasse in Canada – European crevasses are smaller than this

7 Look at Photo 1.7 and read the text on crevasses.

a What does a crevasse look like?

b How deep are the biggest crevasses and where are they found?

c Describe how crevasses are formed. Use a sketch (see Figure 1.6, page 71) to help illustrate your description.

8 You have been asked to design a simple poster to be displayed in a car park close to a glacier. Many tourists visit the glacier and some even clamber on the ice. Last year a teenager fell down a crevasse and broke both his legs. Your poster needs to inform people of the dangers of walking on the ice. Use sketches to illustrate the dangers.

The glacier is in France but it is visited by many British tourists. Either avoid words completely and use just symbols, or use both English and French words.

2 Ice in the past

Look back to Photo 1.2, page 69. Just 18 000 years ago, mountains throughout most of Europe, would have looked similar to the present-day Alps. **Ice sheets**, several kilometres thick, spread down from the north as the climate cooled. Massive **icebergs** floated in the Atlantic Ocean (see Figure 2.1). In addition to the great ice sheets, glaciers filled and eroded the valleys. The period of time when ice covered much of Europe is called the **Ice Age**.

Today the ice sheets have retreated and there are only pockets of ice left, for example, in the Alps and in the mountains of Sweden and Norway. Further north, in Iceland, there is much more ice because the climate is still very cold.

1 For this activity you will need an outline map of Europe.

a Make a careful copy of Figure 2.1.

b Use Atlas Map B, page 11, to identify and then label the two mountain ranges in southern Europe.

c Use Atlas Map A, page 10, to discover the countries that were under ice during the Ice Age. Label these on your map.

d Use Atlas Map B, to name the area that is labelled 'main centre' on Figure 2.1.

e What are icebergs and where were they found during the Ice Age?

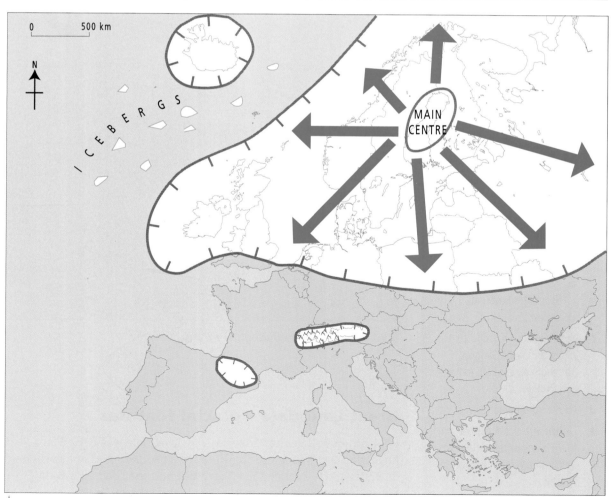

▲ *2.1 The maximum advance of ice during the Ice Age*

Case study: Ice in the British Isles

There are no glaciers in the British Isles today, but they have left their mark on our landscape. Much of the dramatic mountain scenery of Scotland, the Welsh mountains and the Lake District was formed by ice sheets and glaciers during the Ice Age.

Figure 2.2 shows what happened in more detail. Notice that the country was affected by a huge ice sheet from Scandinavia. In addition, many smaller glaciers spread out from the major mountain ranges.

---

2 You will need an outline map of the British Isles for this activity

a Make a copy of Figure 2.2 on your map.

b Name the four mountain ranges. Choose from the following list:
- Grampian Mountains (northern Scotland)
- Lake District (England)
- Southern Uplands (southern Scotland)
- Snowdonia (North Wales).

c Use Atlas Map A, page 10, to locate and label Glasgow, Birmingham, London, Belfast and Dublin.

d Locate your home town or city.

e Discuss as a class whether there is any evidence that your home area was once affected by ice.

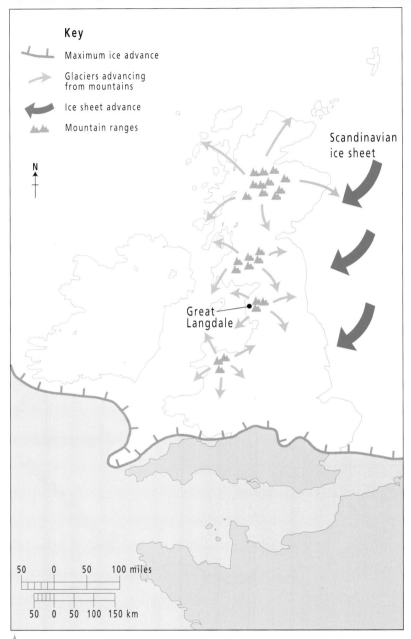

▲ *2.2 The British Isles during the Ice Age*

Great Langdale – glacial features

Look at Photo 2.3. The valley of Great Langdale was carved by a huge glacier in much the same way that the Mer de Glace is carving its valley today. Notice the steep sides and the broad, flat valley floor. A valley like this one is called a **glacial trough**. It is also sometimes known as a **U-shaped valley** because of its shape.

3 Look at Photo 2.3.

a Write a few sentences describing the landscape of the Lake District. Use some of the following words to help you.

- bleak • dramatic • mountainous • forested
- fields • steep sides • flat valley floor
- bare rock • exposed • wild.

b Does this type of landscape appeal to you? Give reasons for your answer.

c Landscapes such as the one shown in Photo 2.3 are popular with tourists. What activities can tourists do in these areas?

4 Look at Photo 2.3.

a Can you see any towns or large villages in the photo?

b Where are the buildings to be found? (They appear white in the photo.)

c What is the land used for on the valley floor at A?

d Try to suggest what sort of farming is likely to take place on the open moorland at B.

e What is the land used for at C?

f Why do you think the valley floor is most suitable for farming?

▲ *2.3 Great Langdale Valley in the Lake District (see location on Figure 2.2)*

Corries and tarns

Look closely at Photo 2.3. Try to spot the deep hollow on the far side of the valley perched up on the hillside. You can see another view of this feature in Photo 2.4. It is a **corrie**.

A corrie is formed when a great thickness of ice scoops out the rock on a hillside, rather like the action of an ice-cream scoop (see Figure 2.5). Thousands of years of grinding and scraping eventually create the deep depression you can see in Photos 2.3 and 2.4. Rainwater may be stored within the hollow to form a lake such as Stickle Tarn.

2.4 Corries are very common landforms in glaciated areas. They often have a lake called a tarn in the bottom of them. This one is called Stickle Tarn.

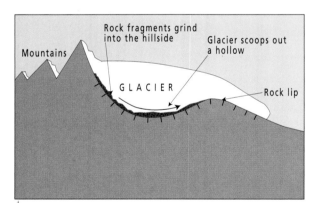

2.5 The formation of a corrie

5 Study Figure 2.5. Describe with the aid of a simple diagram how a corrie is formed.

6 Make a copy of Figure 2.6. Add the following labels in their correct places, using Photo 2.4 to help you:
   - steep, rocky back wall
   - deep hollow
   - lake (Stickle Tarn)
   - steep-sided river valley
   - Great Langdale Valley.

2.6 Sketch of Stickle Tarn corrie

3 Enquiry: Avalanche!

You may wish to use the information in this Enquiry to produce a longer project on Avalanches or, alternatively, you can work through the activities at the end of each box. The Internet is an excellent source of information about avalanches.

ENQUIRY A

What is an avalanche?

An **avalanche** is a mass of snow and ice that moves very rapidly down a mountainside (see Photo 3.1). They are very sudden events and rarely last more than a few minutes. Avalanches are tremendously powerful as the weight of snow and ice combines with debris such as rocks and trees. People caught in an avalanche often describe it as sounding like an oncoming train.

Most avalanches occur on steep slopes and in the spring. Melting weakens the layers of snow and ice causing them to become unstable. A small earthquake, or even people skiing or snowboarding, can trigger the sudden collapse that leads to an avalanche (see Figure 3.2).

▲ *3.1 An avalanche*

▼ *3.2 Factors that make an avalanche likely to occur*

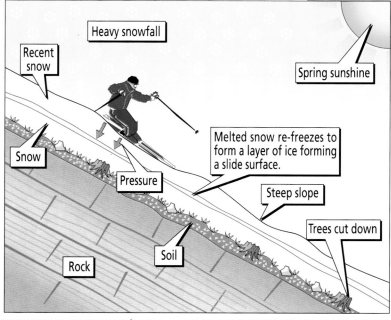

Heavy snowfall

Recent snow

Spring sunshine

Snow

Melted snow re-freezes to form a layer of ice forming a slide surface.

Pressure

Steep slope

Trees cut down

Soil

Rock

1 Study Figure 3.2.

a Describe, with the help of a diagram, the factors that increase the risk of avalanches.

b Give an example of a natural trigger event.

c Give two examples of human activity that can trigger avalanches.

What are the effects of avalanches?

Every year avalanches claim hundreds of lives across the world. They also destroy houses, bridges and roads. Look at Table 3.3. Notice that the majority of the deaths in Europe occurred in only four countries.

On 23 January, 1998, a group of school children were caught by an avalanche near the ski resort of Les Orres in the French Alps. Nine children and two adult guides were killed. It was the worst avalanche disaster in France since 1970. On 23 February 1999 heavy snowfall triggered a massive avalanche which engulfed the Austrian ski resort of Galtür (see Figures 3.4/3.5).

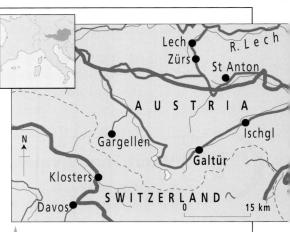

3.4 Location map of Galtür

Country	No. of people killed
Switzerland	24
France	23
Austria	27
Italy	13
Germany	4
Slovakia	2
Spain	4
Norway	4
Poland	5
Bulgaria	4

◀ 3.3 Deaths from avalanches in Europe, 1997

3.5 Report of the disaster at Galtür, 23 February, 1999

INNSBRUCK, Austria (AP) – Tons of snow tumbled down upon a small village in the Austrian Alps on Tuesday, killing at least eight people and leaving up to 30 others missing. It was one of dozens of avalanches to strike central Europe as the region endured its worst snowfall in 50 years.

Tens of thousands of travellers were stranded in train stations, traffic jams and isolated resort towns across France, Switzerland, Italy and Austria as the avalanches buried homes, roads and railways.

Tuesday's avalanche struck shortly after 4 p.m. in Galtür, an Austrian town in the Paznaun Valley near the Swiss border.

'We were drinking hot mulled wine, when suddenly it started. The lights went out. It was dark. There was only dust and snow. We got out of there as fast as we could,' Franz Wenko, a hotel operator in the town told Austrian television.

Residents managed to dig out about 20 people, but Austrian television said that an estimated 25 to 30 more were still buried as night fell. Some of those rescued were reported to be critically injured.

No outside help has reached Galtür, a town of 700, because an earlier avalanche had blocked the main road into it and bad weather prevented helicopters in, said Austrian Army maj. Wartok, who declined to give his first name.

Snow was falling heavily Tuesday night, with another 20 inches expected by morning, the Austrian Press Agency said. The army and other rescuers put off attempts to reach Galtür until Wednesday.

Wartok told The Associated Press that many of the missing were assumed to be trapped in houses buried in the avalanche. He said that people trapped in houses have a better chance of surviving than those caught in the open, where the heavy weight of the snow soon suffocates them.

1 You will need an outline map of Europe for this activity.

a Present the information in Table 3.3 as a series of proportional bars on your map. Make sure you follow the tips below:
- Take time to work out your vertical scale.
- Keep your bars a constant width.
- Try to place each bar with its base in the right country.
- Give your map a title and explain your scale in a key.

b Turn to Atlas Map B, page 11. What do you notice about the countries recording the greatest number of deaths?

2 Use Figures 3.4 and 3.5 to write a newspaper front page article about the Austrian avalanche disaster. Use pictures or sketches of avalanches if you wish. Encyclopedia CD-ROMs are very good sources of photos, as is the Internet.

ENQUIRY C

Can the hazard of avalanches be reduced?

Most areas at risk from avalanches, particularly in ski resorts, have a system of avalanche warnings. Teams of experts monitor the state of the snow and keep a careful eye on the weather. Warnings can then be issued for areas thought to be at risk.

Avalanches can be made less likely by the building of wooden fences on a slope to hold back the snow (see Figure 3.6). Trees can also help prevent avalanches starting because they hold the snow pack together. Trees will also break up smaller avalanches, preventing them from becoming too dangerous. Roads and buildings that are at risk from avalanches can have shutes built to help protect them.

1 Study Figure 3.6. It shows some forms of avalanche protection on the hills above the small fictional village of Blumenkold in Austria.

a Make a careful copy of Figure 3.6, using colours to make your sketch clear and attractive.

b Add the following labels in their correct places on your diagram

- Avalanche shed to protect railway line.
- Fences on the steep slopes to hold the snow.
- Newly-planted trees to hold snow and break up small avalanches.
- Wedges to protect electricity pylons.
- Mounds to slow down any avalanche as it hits flatter ground.
- Walls on the steep slopes to hold the snow.

c Choose any three forms of protection and explain in detail how each one helps to reduce the dangers of avalanches.

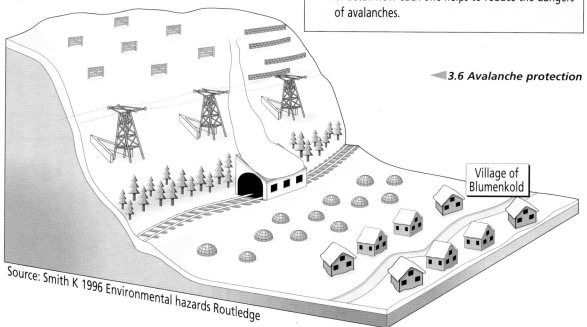

◀ *3.6 Avalanche protection*

Village of Blumenkold

Source: Smith K 1996 Environmental hazards Routledge

Web search

There are several good Internet sites dealing with avalanches. Try a general search using the word 'avalanche' or visit these sites:

- The Cyberspace Snow and Avalanche Center, www.csac.org/ reports incidents and provides video footage and statistics

- The Scottish Avalanche Information Service, www.sais.gov.uk/ reports and gives warnings of possible avalanches in the Scottish mountains.

Water

Water is vital for life. It is used in our homes for drinking, cooking, and washing. Industries use it for processing materials and generating power. Farmers need it to grow food and support livestock. In the UK, water always seems to be available at the turn of a tap, but in some parts of the world it is in very short supply. Water is a resource that needs to be carefully managed. Where does it come from and how does it reach our homes?

1 The water cycle

Where is all the water?

The air above our heads is called the **atmosphere**. The atmosphere consists mainly of gases like oxygen and nitrogen but it also contains water.

However, most water (over 97 per cent) is found in the world's oceans. The rest is found on land.

Water is constantly on the move between the atmosphere, the oceans and the land. This movement is called the **water cycle**. Look at Figure 1.1 and read the following text to find out how water moves around the world.

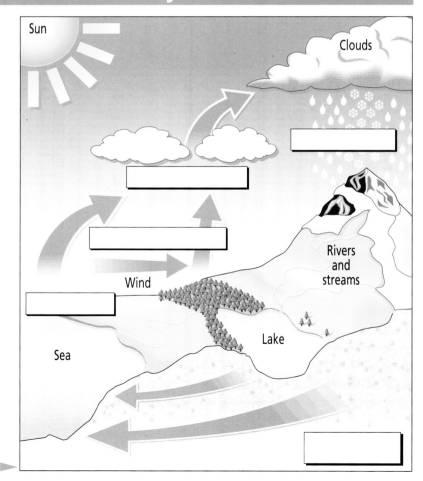

1.1 The water cycle

▲ *1.2 Clouds building up on a hot summer's day*

The stages of the water cycle

Water falls to the ground as **precipitation**. This is usually in the form of rain but it can include snow, sleet and hail. Most rain falls directly into the oceans, because they cover 70 per cent of the Earth's surface. Water that falls on land often flows over the ground as streams and rivers. It eventually makes its way to the sea. Some rainwater will, however, soak into the soil and pass very slowly through the rocks as **groundwater flow**.

Water on the Earth's surface is passed into the atmosphere by a process called **evaporation**. This process is invisible – liquid water, such as water that you find in a puddle, turns into water vapour as it passes into the air. Although we cannot see evaporation taking place, we do notice its effects when puddles and pavements dry up after it has rained.

On land, plants and trees take up water through their roots in order to grow. Some of this water is returned to the air from the leaves by a process called **transpiration**. Once in the air, the water vapour rises and cools. As it cools, it begins to **condense**, turning it from a vapour, back into water droplets to form clouds. The clouds steadily grow in size, and soon the water droplets fall back to Earth as precipitation (see Photo 1.2). The cycle has now come full circle.

---

1 Make a copy of Figure 1.1. Write the following labels in their correct boxes to describe what is happening:

- Groundwater flow
- Transpiration from plants
- Precipitation, e.g. rain and snow
- Condensation forming clouds
- Evaporation from the sea.

2 Write out the following sentences, selecting the correct words from the list below.

Water is constantly moving from the _____ to the Earth and back again. This is called the water _____ . Most water reaches the Earth's surface as _____ where it either_____ as rivers, or soaks into the _____ . Eventually most water flows into the _____ . Water passes into the air by a process called _____ which turns liquid water into water vapour. Condensation then occurs as the air cools and _____ are formed.

rain flows trees clouds atmosphere
soil frozen evaporation cycle sea canal

2 Water supply in Spain

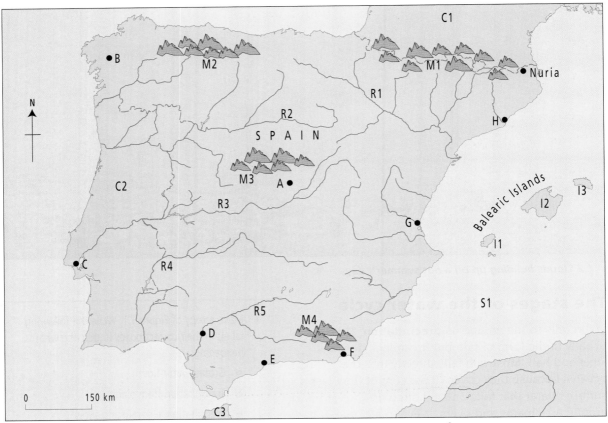

2.1 General geography of Spain

Spain is one of the largest countries in Europe. It is twice the size of the UK. Much of Spain is made up of high ground. In Europe, it is second only to Switzerland, in its average height above sea level. Before continuing, let's discover more about the basic geography of Spain.

1 Look at Atlas Map C, opposite.

a Notice that most of Spain is coloured yellow or brown. Look at the key and write a sentence to explain what these colours tell us about Spain.

b What are the names of the two major mountain ranges in northern Spain?

c What is the name of Spain's highest mountain peak?
 ● What height is it above sea level?

d Name the two European countries which border Spain.

e Find Gibraltar at the southern tip of Spain. To which country does Gibraltar belong?

f The Strait of Gibraltar separates Spain from which north African country?

g What is the capital of Spain?

h Which city, after Madrid, has the largest population? (Look at the key to identify the correct symbol to search for.)
 ● Where is this city located?

2 For this activity you will need to make a copy of Figure 2.1. Use Atlas Map C, opposite, to help you complete your map by naming the following in a key below your map:

a Countries, C1 – C3

b Mountain ranges, M1 – M4

c Rivers, R1 – R5

d Towns, A – H

e Sea, S1

f Islands, 1 – 3.

The rain in Spain ...

Have you heard the saying 'The rain in Spain falls mainly on the plain...'? In fact, although much of Spain is a high plateau or 'plain' (see Photo 2.2), the highest rainfall occurs over the mountains in the north (see Photo 2.3).

Rainfall patterns

Look at Figure 2.4 on the opposite page. There is a great variation in the amount of rainfall across Spain. Rainfall is highest in the north and west, and lowest in central and southern parts. Winters in Spain tend to be wet and summers very dry.

Table 2.5 records the rainfall during the year for Santiago in the north-west and Almeria in the south-east.

The pattern of rainfall in Spain creates two major problems for water supply:
● There is a regional imbalance, with high amounts of rainfall in the north and west of Spain, but low amounts in the centre and south.
● Whilst there is usually enough rain in the winter, there can be shortages in the summer. In addition, the summers are very hot so much of the rain that does fall is lost through evaporation.

◄ *2.2 The high plains of central Spain*

2.3 Most rain falls in the mountain areas of northern Spain ▼

3 Study Figure 2.4. Write a few sentences describing the pattern of rainfall shown.

4 Draw two rainfall bar graphs, one above the other, to show the information in Table 2.5. Give your graphs a title and make sure the axes are labelled. Then work through the steps below.

a Draw up a table to record the highest and lowest average monthly rainfalls for Santiago and Almeria. Record both the name of the month and the amount of rain in your table.

b Calculate the average total rainfall for the year for both places.

c What do your bar graphs tell you about the difference in rainfall between the north-west of Spain and the south-east?

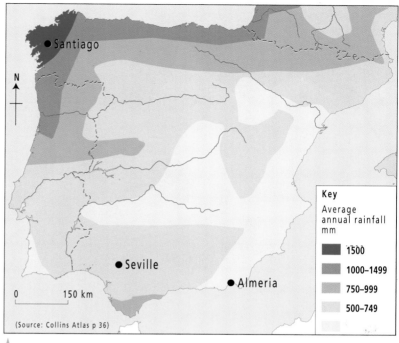

2.4 Most rain falls in the mountain areas of northern Spain

2.5 Average monthly rainfall

	J	F	M	A	M	J	J	A	S	O	N	D
Santiago (mm)	203	136	175	108	107	64	38	49	51	117	191	178
Almeria (mm)	31	21	20	28	17	4	0.5	5	15	26	27	36

Demand for water in Spain

The demand for water is very high in central and south-eastern Spain. These areas have very low rainfall and maintaining a steady water supply is extremely difficult.

Farming

Much of Spain's farmland relies upon **irrigation**, particularly in the summer. Over three million hectares of land is irrigated. Irrigation is essential for cultivating fruit crops, such as oranges, and vegetables (see Photo 2.6).

2.6 The hot climate in the south, helps to ripen the crops quickly, but they also need large quantities of water to grow

WATER

▲ *2.7 Tourist developments, such as this water park in southern Spain, increase the water problems of the region*

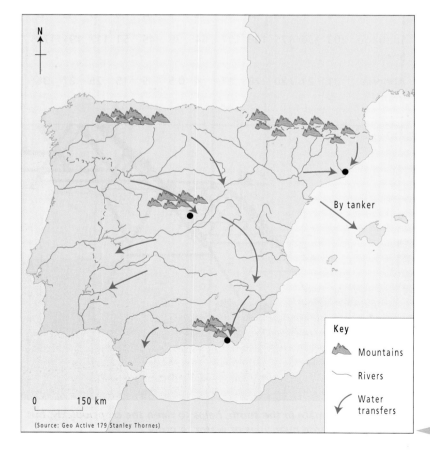

Key

⛰ Mountains

〜 Rivers

↙ Water transfers

0   150 km

(Source: Geo Active 179 Stanley Thornes)

Tourism

Over 50 million tourists visit Spain each year (see Photo 2.7). Most travel to the Mediterranean coast, where they increase the demand for fresh water in an area which is already very dry. Some resorts ration water by turning it off for part of the day.

Managing water in Spain

There are two main ways in which water is being managed in Spain:

● **Increasing water supplies** – There are a number of water transfer schemes (see Figure 2.8) which generally take water from the north and west to the centre and south of the country. In mainland Spain, water is moved by canals, aqueducts and pipelines. New reservoirs are also being built in the mountains to store water for summer use.

On the island of Mallorca, water is imported by tanker. This water is taken from the River Ebro on the mainland (see Atlas Map C, page 83). This scheme, which began in 1995, is not popular with the people on the mainland as they are also short of water. For the future, the island is promised a desalination plant which will convert seawater to freshwater.

● **Encouraging water conservation** – People are urged to conserve water and not to be so wasteful with it. Farmers are beginning to use

◀ *2.8 Water transfers in Spain*

trickle irrigation, rather than spray irrigation which is far less wasteful. Many golf course are watering their greens and fairways with waste water.

Even with these measures some areas of Spain suffer from severe water shortages during the summer months. In addition, near the coast, underground water levels are so low that seawater is beginning to pollute the freshwater.

5 You will need a blank outline of Spain for this activity.

a Make a copy of Figure 2.8. (Use a bold colour to show the water transfers.)

b Use Atlas Map C, page 83, to label:
- the main rivers on your map
- the three cities X, Y and Z
- the island of Mallorca.

c How is water transferred from:
- the north of Spain to the south
- mainland Spain to Mallorca?

d Why are some people unhappy about water from the mainland being sent to Mallorca?

e How does Mallorca hope to obtain water in the future?

6 Summer is the season in which water shortages are at their worst.

a Which two groups of people start using more water at this time of year?

b Design a poster, to be displayed in hotels on the Costa del Sol, outlining four or five simple ways in which tourists can save water.

c As a class, discuss how you would feel if your were asked to save water on holiday. Would you mind the water being cut off for certain periods of the day?

3 Water pollution

Water **pollution** is one of the most widespread threats to our natural environment. When harmful chemicals leak into rivers (Figure 3.1), the entire ecosystem can be affected. Fish die and other forms of wildlife are damaged. Figure 3.2 on page 88 describes some of the effects of a chemical spill on the River Ellen in the UK. (Look back to page 31 to remind you about the 1986 incident on the River Rhine.)

1 Look at Photo 3. 1.

a What is the cause of the pollution shown in the photo?

b The word pollution means 'to make foul'. Do you think that, with reference to the photo, this is a good definition? Why?

▲ *3.1 Waste from a chemical factory being discharged into the River Mersey, UK*

CAUSTIC SODA SPILL IN RIVER KILLS THOUSANDS OF FISH

Thousands of fish, including migratory salmon and trout, have died after caustic soda spilt into a Cumbrian river.

People were warned yesterday to avoid touching the polluted water, which can burn the skin. Wildlife experts fear widespread harm to breeding birds that need clean water, such as dippers and kingfishers and colonies of otters that feed on eels in the lower reaches.

The Ellen pollution emerged on Monday night and swept down a ten-mile stretch into the harbour at Maryport yesterday. Investigators with the National River Authority and the Agriculture Ministry have linked the incident with a creamery at Aspatria owned by Dairy Crest, where the chemical is used to clean milk vats and neutralise effluent. They believe the chemical leaked from a storage tank.

James Carr, of the Salmon and Trout Association, said members were pulling dead fish out by the bucketful. 'The Ellen is one of those very rare things, a small, beautiful river.'

2 Study Figure 3.2. Use the information to design a front page spread for the local newspaper. You have been told by your editor that you only have space for 120 words. Make your account as hard-hitting as you can.

◄ *3.2*

▼ *3.3 Causes of water pollution*

Aquifers

Water held in rocks underground can also be polluted, for example, by chemicals used in farming. Rainwater, seeping through the soil, carries the harmful chemicals into the underlying rocks. The rainwater moves down and eventually contaminates underground stores of water. Water from these reservoirs, or **aquifers** as they are known, then has to be treated at great expense before it is safe to drink.

Figure 3.3 looks at some more causes of water pollution. (Pollution of the sea is another serious type of water pollution. We will be looking at this in Book 3.)

Reducing water pollution

Throughout Europe, government agencies monitor the quality of surface and underground water. Regular checks are carried out and polluters can be fined. If a pollution incident occurs, scientists act quickly to reduce the effects and protect wildlife. People, who wish to discharge waste into rivers, have to obtain permission to do so, and their emissions are monitored.

There are a number of practical measures that can be taken to prevent pollution. The vast majority of waste water, including sewage, is treated before it is allowed to enter rivers or the sea. One method used to catch solid objects and prevent then being washed downstream is to construct metal grids called **trash screens** across a river. In some countries, farmers are encouraged to use fewer chemicals on the soil in order to reduce the pollution of aquifers.

3 Look at Figure 3.3.

a How can power stations pollute rivers?

b Give an example of an industry which discharges chemical waste into rivers.

c Can you find two sources of oil pollution?

4 Make a copy of the sketch in Figure 3.4. Use the information in Figure 3.3, pages 88–89, to help you complete the sketch by labelling the five causes of water pollution shown.

5 Figure 3.5 is a sketch of a farm. There are several sources of pollution on the farm.

a Make a copy of Figure 3.5. Add labels to identify the pollution hazards.

b For each hazard, suggest what could be done to prevent it causing pollution in the future.

6 As a class, discuss ways of reducing water pollution. Are there stretches of water in your home area that would benefit from being cleaned up?
● Who or what is responsible for polluting them?
● Would it be worthwhile to install trash screens?
● What can be done to make people more aware of water pollution?

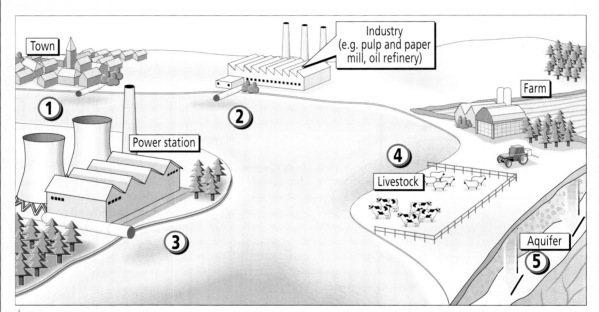

3.4 Sources of water pollution

3.5 Sources of pollution on a farm

France

France is the largest country in Western Europe. It was one of the founding members of the EU. France has a very varied landscape with thousands of kilometres of coastline, mountains and even extinct volcanoes. Its landscape offers great opportunities for energy generation, farming and for tourism. There are many special environments in France, for example the wetlands of the Camargue.

1 A tour of France

In this unit you will get to know more about the basic geography of France. It is a vast country and it is important that you have an understanding of where things are in order that you can develop a sense of place. Turn to Atlas Map D, page 93, and find the Alps, the Mediterranean and the capital city, Paris. Look for other places that you may have heard about or perhaps even visisted.

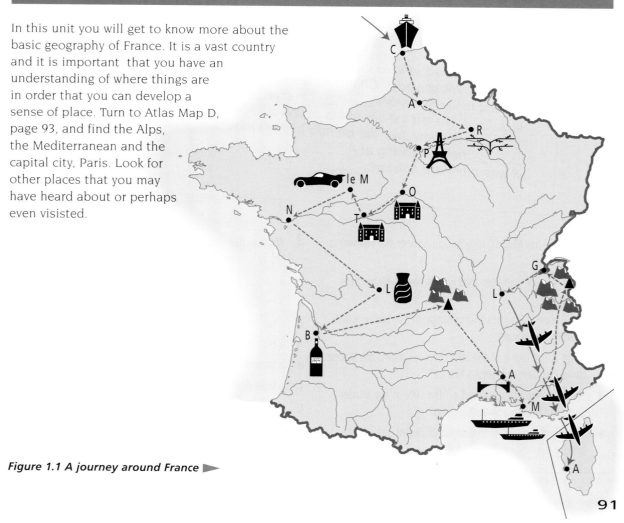

Figure 1.1 A journey around France ▶

1 Figure 1.1, page 91, shows the route taken during a trip to France. Use Atlas Map D, opposite, to help you complete the spaces, numbered 1–21, in the following account. All the towns and cities have their initial letters written on Figure 1.1.

We arrived at Calais on the ferry and drove to the town of A_____ 1 . We then travelled to R_____ 2 to see some Champagne vineyards. Next stop, P_____ 3 , where we visited several museums (boring!), took a boat trip on the River _____ 4 , and went up the Eiffel Tower (wicked!). We then travelled south to O_____ 5 where we drove alongside the River _____ 6 to the town of T_____ 7 . There were some impressive looking chateaux on the river. Next we headed north to le M_____ 8 , the town made famous by its 24-hour car race. From here we drove to N_____ 9 . A long drive inland ended up at L_____ 10 where Mum bought some local pottery. Then on to B_____ 11 on the River _____ 12 so that Dad could buy some wine called claret (yuk!).
We next visited the Massif Central mountains and climbed the highest peak called Mt Dore. It is _____ 13 metres high. Then we drove south-east to the town of A_____ 14 on the River _____ 15 . Here we went "sur le pont ..." as the song goes. We then spent some time in M_____ 16 at the harbour. There were some splendid boats there.
We then drove inland to the French Alps which were really beautiful. We stayed at Chamonix where we could see France's highest mountain, Mont _____ 17 . On then to _____ 18 and L_____ 19 . We left the car at the airport and flew to the island of _____ 20 . We flew over the island's highest mountain, called _____ 21 before landing at A_____ 22 .
It was a brilliant holiday!

2 Look at Atlas Map D, to help you answer the following questions.

a Name the six countries that France shares its borders with.

b The Rhône is France's fourth longest river but in which country is its source?

c What is the name of the lake through which the Rhône flows just before it enters France?

d Which major city is located on the lake at the border between France and Switzerland?

e What is the name of the river that forms part of the border between France and Germany?

3 Work in pairs to try to name one French example of the following:

a a perfume manufacturer

b a footballer playing in the English Premier League

c a car manufacturer

d a type of wine

e a famous building in Paris (not the Eiffel Tower)

f a type of food

g a French word that that has become part of the English language.

Now, compare your answers with the rest of the class.

FRANCE

BELGIUM

GERMA

LUXEMBOURG

FRANCE

SPAIN

ANDORRA

SWITZERLAND

ITALY

MONACO

English Channel

Channel Islands (UK)

Baie de la Seine

Normandy

Brittany

Picardie

Ardennes

Bay of Biscay

Biscay

Gulf of Gascony

Touraine

Limousin

Massif Central

Dauphine

Alpes Maritimes

Côte d'Azur

Ligurian Sea

Gulf of Lions

Gulf of Genoa

Languedoc

PYRÉNÉES

Corsica (France)

Sardinia (Italy)

KEY

Relief metres	
5000	
3000	
2000	
1000	
500	
200	
sea level	

Permanent ice

4808 ▲ Mountain height (in metres)

〜 River

⋯ Intermittent river

Canal

Lake / Reservoir

Marsh

─── International boundary

■ Capital city

● Large town or city

○ Other town or city

SCALE 1 : 5 750 000

0   50   100   150   200 km

FRANCE

▼ 1.2 Facts about France

France has a population of 57 million, about the same as the UK. 9 million people live in Paris. France covers 54 000 km² – it is more than twice the size of the UK.

France has four major rivers. The Loire, over 1000 km in length, is the longest. The others are the Seine (770 km), the Garonne (650 km), and the Rhône (522 km in France).

Mont Blanc in the French Alps is the highest mountain in Western Europe (4807 metres). The Pyrenees form the border between France and Spain.

France has a varied climate: the south of the country has a Mediterranean climate with hot, dry summers and mild winters. The western coast receives high amounts of rainfall. The north has hot summers but cool winters. The mountains are high enough for snow and ice to remain all year round.

A huge range of crops is grown including fruit, cereals and vegetables. Forests make up 28 per cent of the country. They provide wood for furniture and paper manufacturing. Most raw materials have to be imported as France does not have large reserves of minerals (such as iron ore, copper, and tin) or fuels (such as oil and coal).

In 1994 the Channel Tunnel opened, linking France to the UK. In 1997, nearly 2.5 million cars were carried through the tunnel by Eurostar trains.

France was a major colonial power. Today, French is spoken in several African countries including Algeria, Niger, Zaire and Mauritania.

Most large French companies have their headquarters in Paris. The government is based there. Paris is regarded as France's cultural centre with museums, cathedrals and the Eiffel Tower.

In 1998, France won the World Cup, beating Brazil 3-0 in the final.

France's main industries are micro-electronics, aerospace and car manufacturing.

4 Use the information in Figure 1.2 and what you have already learnt in this unit, to help you produce a poster about France. Use sketches, diagrams and pictures to illustrate your poster. (You could include labels and wrappers from supermarket products too.) Find additional information about France in encyclopedias or on the Internet if you have access to it.

2 Energy in France

France has very little fossil fuel. There is some coal in the north-east of the country (see Figure 2.1) but production has fallen greatly in recent years. France does not have any of its own oil. It has to import it by tanker from the Middle East, the UK and Norway. There is some natural gas in the south-west but not very much. Hydro-electric power (HEP) is produced on some of France's major rivers, for example, on the River Isère in the Alps.

Look at Table 2.2. It shows the different sources of energy used in France. Unlike other countries in Europe, nuclear power is a major source of energy.

▼ **2.2**

Energy use in France, 1996	(%)
Oil	40.5
Coal	6.6
Gas	13.6
Nuclear	31.9
HEP	5.6
Solar, tidal etc	1.8
Total	100 %

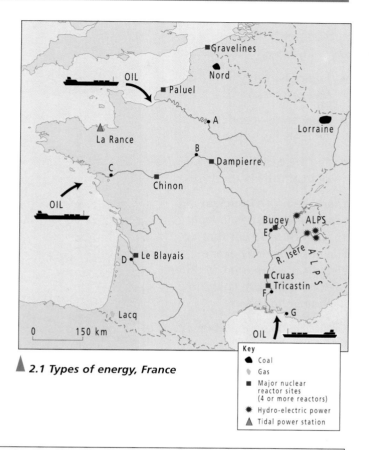

▲ **2.1 Types of energy, France**

Key
● Coal
◆ Gas
■ Major nuclear reactor sites (4 or more reactors)
✳ Hydro-electric power
▲ Tidal power station

1 You will need a blank outline map of France for this activity.

a Make a copy of Figure 2.1.

b Use Atlas Map D, page 93, to help you label the cities A-G.

c The following rivers have been drawn on Figure 2.1. Use the the atlas map to identify them and then label them on your map:
- Loire
- Rhône
- Seine
- Garonne.

2 Study Figure 2.1 and Atlas Map D, page 93, or use the map you completed for Activity 1, to answer the following questions.

a On which river are the greatest number of major nuclear power sites?

b Which nuclear power site is found close to the city of Bordeaux?

c Which nuclear power site is closest to the UK?

d How many kilometres is the Dampierre nuclear power site from Paris?

e What are the names of the two coalfields?

f What type of energy is produced in the Alps?

g What form of energy enters France through the port of Marseilles?

3 Look at Table 2.2.

a Present the information in the form of a pie chart (remember to multiply the percentage figures by 3.6 to give you degrees).

b What were the two main types of energy used in France in 1996?

c What percentage of France's energy came from fossil fuels in 1996?

Nuclear power

In the 1970s, the French government decided to develop nuclear power. There were several reasons for this decision:

- France had very little fossil fuel of its own

- France was very dependent on fuels from abroad

- the price of oil increased dramatically in the 1970s.

There are now 57 **nuclear reactors** at 21 sites in France. They produce 75 per cent of France's electricity. Some electricity is exported by cable to other European countries, including the UK.

One of the main requirements for a nuclear reactor is water. This is why nuclear power stations are located on rivers or close to the sea. Large amounts of water is needed to cool the reactor and to produce the steam which turns the turbines to produce the electricity. Look at Figure 2.4.

2.3 A nuclear power station in France

2.4 How a pressurised water reactor generates electricity

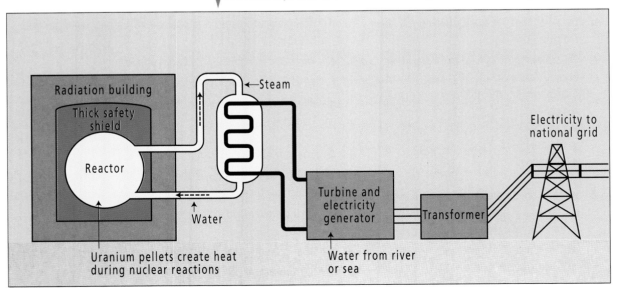

96

Arguments against nuclear power

Nuclear power is a controversial form of energy, although most French people support its use. Some people, however, are concerned about the dangers of **radioactive leaks**. Leaks are extremely hazardous – in 1986, the Chernobyl reactor, near Kiev in Russia, exploded, sending radioactive debris over much of northern Europe, including the UK. Land and food were contaminated. Many people died and children are still being born today around Kiev with terrible deformities and illnesses. This accident made people realise that nuclear reactors pose a risk to the whole of Europe and not just to the country in which they are located.

Radioactive waste

Another issue that concerns all of Europe is what should be done with radioactive waste? Part of the waste from nuclear power stations will be highly toxic for thousands of years – how should it be disposed of? Is it safe to dump underground or deep down in the sea? Some people believe that we should stop using nuclear power until we have discovered a safe way of dealing with the waste.

Governments are also concerned about terrorists obtaining radioactive material and using it to threaten or harm people.

Arguments for nuclear power

Nuclear power uses very little raw fuel (**uranium**). Uranium reserves should last much longer than coal or oil. Some of the spent fuel can actually be re-used. In addition, the every-day emissions from a nuclear power station are far less damaging to the environment that than those from coal and oil-fired power stations.

---

4 Re-read the information on nuclear power.

a Why did France decide to develop nuclear power as a major source of energy?

b What proportion of France's electricity is produced by nuclear power?

c Why do nuclear reactors need large amounts of water?

5 Study Figure 2.4.

a Make a copy of the diagram.

b Copy the following paragraph and fill in the spaces, choosing from the words below.

The fuel that is used to create the nuclear reactions and the supply of heat is called _____. The nuclear reactions take place in the _____ which is housed in the radiation building. _____ is used to cool the reactor and also to produce steam. It is the steam that generates the _____. This is then transferred to the _____ grid to supply homes and industry.

**electricity   solar   national   transformer
reactor   water   limestone   uranium**

6 Look at Figure 2.5.

a Make a copy of the diagram and complete the empty boxes by writing some advantages and disadvantages of nuclear power.

b Do you think nuclear power is a good idea? Give reasons for your answer. If you want to research this further, you could visit one of these Internet sites:
British Nuclear Fuels www.bnfl.com./ns-home.html
Friends of the Earth www.foe.co.uk
Greenpeace www.greenpeace.org.uk

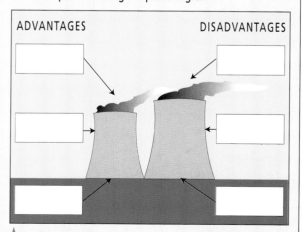

▲ **2.5 Advantages and disadvantages of nuclear power**

FRANCE

La Rance tidal power station

France is home to the biggest **tidal power** plant in the world. It is situated on the River Rance in Brittany, close to St Malo (see Photo 2.6). Built in 1966, it now provides about 8 per cent of Brittany's electricity. One of the main reasons for the choice of the Rance estuary is the very high **tidal range** (difference in height between high tide and low tide) of over 11 metres.

As Photo 2.6 shows, a barrage (dam) some 700 metres long has been built across the river. Within the barrage are tunnels which contain the turbines that generate electricity. As the tide rises and falls, water passes through the tunnels to turn the turbines. The turbines have been specially designed to be turned by both incoming and outgoing tides. At one end of the barrage is a lock to allow shipping to pass through.

7 You have been asked to produce a small leaflet in English about La Rance tidal power scheme. It will be given to English tourists who are interested in visiting the site. The text on this page, and Figure 2.7, contain information to help you in the production of your leaflet.

Include a location map and illustrations as well as a description of how it works. Take time to plan the layout of your leaflet so that it looks attractive.

2.6 La Rance tidal power station in France

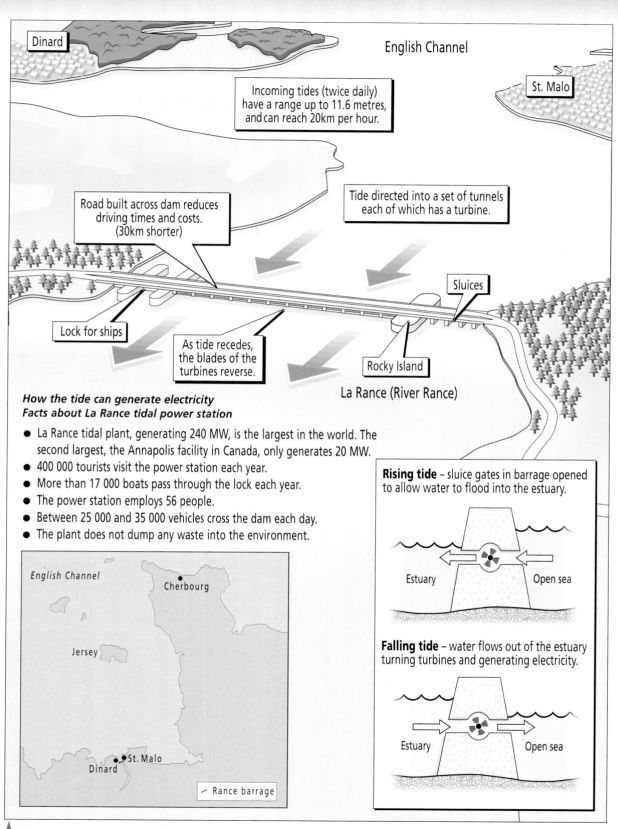

Dinard

English Channel

St. Malo

Incoming tides (twice daily) have a range up to 11.6 metres, and can reach 20km per hour.

Tide directed into a set of tunnels each of which has a turbine.

Road built across dam reduces driving times and costs. (30km shorter)

Sluices

Lock for ships

As tide recedes, the blades of the turbines reverse.

Rocky Island

La Rance (River Rance)

How the tide can generate electricity
Facts about La Rance tidal power station

- La Rance tidal plant, generating 240 MW, is the largest in the world. The second largest, the Annapolis facility in Canada, only generates 20 MW.
- 400 000 tourists visit the power station each year.
- More than 17 000 boats pass through the lock each year.
- The power station employs 56 people.
- Between 25 000 and 35 000 vehicles cross the dam each day.
- The plant does not dump any waste into the environment.

English Channel

Cherbourg

Jersey

St. Malo
Dinard

Rance barrage

Rising tide – sluice gates in barrage opened to allow water to flood into the estuary.

Estuary

Open sea

Falling tide – water flows out of the estuary turning turbines and generating electricity.

Estuary

Open sea

2.7 La Rance tidal power plant

3 Champagne

The Champagne-Ardenne region of France, which is located to the east of Paris, is famous for one thing – its wine. Although wines from other parts of the world may be made in the same way and taste very similar, only those produced in this region of France can bear the name 'Champagne'. The familiar bubbly white wine comes from grapes grown in this region. Most vineyards are centred on the town of Epernay (see Photo 3.1 and Figure 3.2) just to the south of Reims. (Turn to Atlas Map D, page 93, and locate Reims to the north-east of Paris.)

3.1 Vineyards in the Champagne region of France ▶

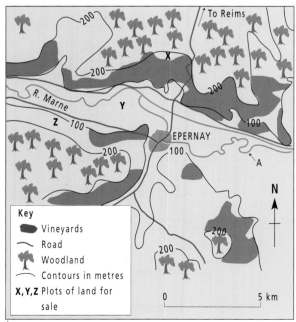

▲ 3.2 Champagne vineyards near Epernay, France

▲ 3.3 Harvesting grapes for Champagne, near Epernay

Why is wine produced in Champagne?

Wine is made from grapes that grow on vines (see Photo 3.3). This type of farming is called **viticulture**. Vines need warm and sunny weather to ripen the grapes in the summer. They also need protection from late spring frosts which can kill the newly forming grapes.

There a several reasons why the Champagne region is well suited to viticulture:

● the soil lies on a rock called **chalk**. Chalk lets water pass through it rather like a sponge does. Rocks that allow this to happen are said to be **permeable**. Grapes grow well in these well drained soils

● the chalk has been excavated to produce ideal cool storage cellars for the millions of bottles of Champagne (see Photo 3.4)

● much of the landscape is gently sloping and the warm and sunny south facing slopes are ideal for growing crops such as vines (see Figure 3.5, page 102)

● late spring frosts are not very common on the slopes where vines are grown, because the cold night air tends to drain away from the slopes down to the valley bottom (see Figure 3.5).

▲ *3.4 There are over 250 km of underground passages in the chalk used for storing Champagne*

1 Study Figure 3.2.

a What is the name of the river that flows through the town of Epernay?

b What river feature is found at A on the map?

c Look at the area of vineyards to the north of the river valley. Notice that the vineyards are on a slope. Between which two contours are most of them found?

d Are the vineyards that are north of the river on a south facing slope or a north facing slope?

e Use Figure 3.5 to help you explain why most of the vineyards are found on the slope to the north of the river.

f What is the main type of land use on the flatter land above the valley side slopes?

2 Look carefully at Figure 3.2 and find the letters X, Y and Z. These are three plots of land that are for sale.

a Using your knowledge about viticulture, suggest which plot would be best suited to become a vineyard. Give reasons for your choice.

b Explain, using simple sketch maps if you wish, why the other two plots are less suitable.

3 Re-read the information on why Champagne is an ideal wine-growing area.

a Chalk is a permeable rock. What does this mean?

b What are the two advantages of chalk for the production of Champagne?

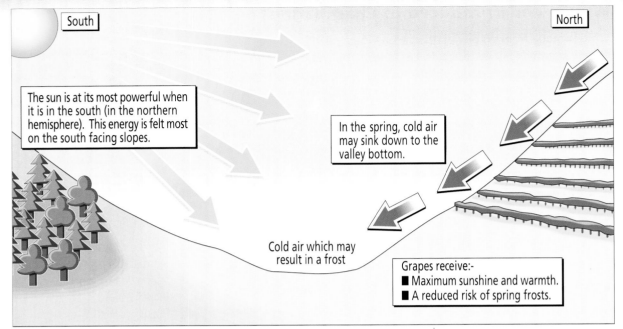

▲ 3.5 South facing slopes protect vines from frost

How does Champagne get its bubbles?

Champagne is sometimes called 'bubbly' on account of its fizziness. After the grapes have been picked, usually in September, they are pressed to extract the juice. It takes about 160 kilos of grapes to produce 100 litres of juice! The juice is then **fermented** to convert the sugar into alcohol.

The next stage in the process involves **blending** (mixing) the new wine with other wines from the area. This is a highly specialised job and is critical in producing the right taste.

The wine is then fermented for a second time. The carbon dioxide produced during this secondary fermentation gives the Champagne its bubbles.

4 Read the information on how Champagne gets its bubbles.

a Make a copy of the diagram in Figure 3.6.

b Put the text in the diagram into the correct boxes.

3.6 The champagne-making process ▼

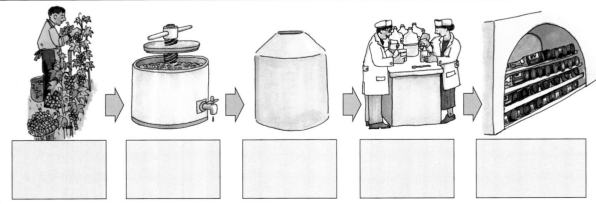

• the grapes are pressed to extract the juice • the grapes are picked in September • the blended wine is bottled and fermented again before being stored • the grapejuice is fermented to turn the sugar into alcohol • the wine is blended with other wines

4 The Camargue

The Camargue is vast area of marshland in the south of France, just to the west of the city of Marseille (see Figure 4.1). It is one of the most important **wetlands** in Europe as it is home to a wide variety of birds, animals and plants.

The Camargue lies at the mouth of France's fourth longest river, the River Rhône. Where the river enters the Mediterranean Sea a **delta** has formed. It is this delta that is the Camargue.

What is a delta?

A delta is a large area of flat or very gently sloping land found where a river joins the sea or a lake. Look at Figure 4.2 to see how a delta is formed.

When a river meets the sea it slows down. This causes the river to drop (deposit) a large amount of its sediment. The sediment, mostly mud and sand, builds out into the sea and soon begins to break the water surface to form new land.

1 You will need an outline map of France for this activity.

a Using Figure 4.1, plot the following:
  - the course of the River Rhône
  - the mountains
  - the Camargue.

Now refer to Atlas Map D, page 93.

b Label the two mountain ranges on your map.

c Locate and name the following towns:
  - Arles
  - Lyon
  - Geneva.

d Name the lake on the border of France and Switzerland

e Give your map a title: 'The location of the Camargue in France'.

2 Make a copy of Figure 4.2 and describe in your own words how a delta forms.

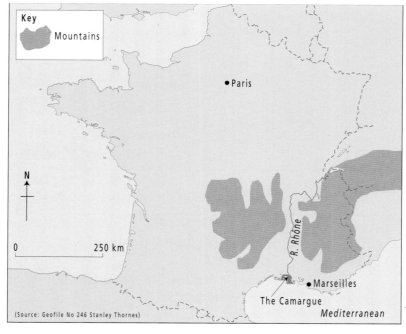

Key
Mountains

• Paris

N

0   250 km

R. Rhône

• Marseilles

The Camargue

Mediterranean

(Source: Geofile No 246 Stanley Thornes)

◀ 4.1 The location of the Camargue, France

River carrying sediment

Sediment deposited at the river mouth builds up to form a delta

Sea

◀ 4.2 The formation of a delta

Look at Figure 4.3. It shows the Rhône delta in more detail. Notice that there are many rivers and lakes on the delta. This is why the area is called a wetland. Notice that the River Rhône splits into two: Le Petit Rhône to the west and Le Grand Rhône to the east. The Camargue is the area in-between these two rivers.

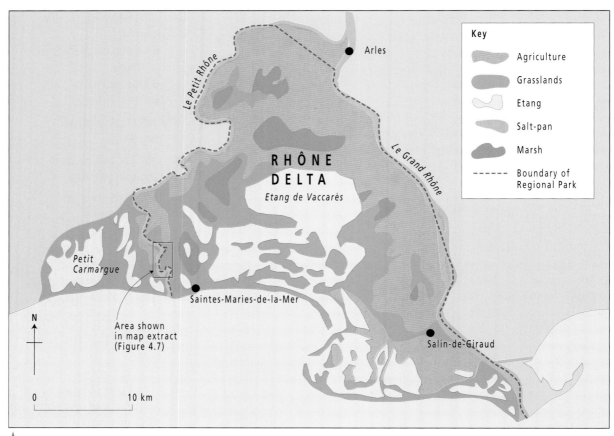

▲ **4.3 Land use in the Carmargue and Rhône delta**

3 Study Figure 4.3.

a What town is situated at the point where the River Rhône splits into two?

b What does the names of the two branches of the River Rhône tell you about the rivers?

c What is an 'etang'?

d What is the name of the large etang on Figure 4.3?

e How wide is this large etang? Name a place roughly the same distance from your home town to give you an idea of its size.

f What is the main land use (apart from etangs) in the Petit Camargue?

g What land use is found to the south of Salin-de-Giraud?

h How far is it from Arles to the coastal town of Saintes-Maries-de-la-Mer?

i In what direction would you be travelling from Arles to Saintes-Maries-de-la-Mer?

j What is the length of the coast between the mouths of the two rivers? (This is a curved line, not a straight line.)

k Why do you think 'Agriculture' is mainly in the north of the area, away from the sea?

What makes the Camargue so special?

At first sight the Camargue seems like a vast, flat wasteland. However, travelling deeper into the centre of the delta, its true beauty is revealed. The many lakes (called **etangs**) are home to huge flocks of birds, in particular, vivid pink flamingoes (see Photo 4.4). The drier land is often a riot of colour, with lavender being especially common. The grasslands are grazed by black bulls, and there are also herds of the famous Camargue white horses (see Photo 4.5).

The Camargue is a special, peaceful place, quite unlike any other part of Europe. It has inspired many writers and painters.

> **4** Look closely at Photos 4.4 and 4.5.
> **a** Describe the landscape of the Camargue.
> **b** Is the landscape attractive to you? Why?

▲ 4.4

▼ 4.5

The Camargue under pressure

The Camargue is under threat from a number of developments.

Farming

In the 19th century, parts of the Camargue were drained to create land for farming, particularly for vineyards. Now there are many kilometres of drainage channels and large parts of the delta are used for growing crops such as wheat and rice. Both crops thrive in the warm conditions typical of southern France in the summer.

The drainage of the land has, however, affected the Camargue ecosystem. Flooding was a natural process and it helped to enrich the soil. It was vital in creating the natural habitats that supported the Camargue wildlife. By draining the land, flooding is now far less common, threatening the survival of some plants and animals.

Salt harvesting

Some of the lakes in the south east of the Camargue, close to Salin-de-Giraud (see Figure 4.3), are artificial. They are, in fact, very shallow lagoons called **salt pans** (see Photo 4.6).

Seawater is pumped into the lagoons where it is left to evaporate in the hot, dry, conditions. Salt is left behind and then harvested. Most of the salt is used in the chemical industry.

▲ 4.6 The Camargue is Europe's largest producer of sea salt

5 Look at Photo 4.6.

a Describe what you can see.

b What impact is salt harvesting having on the landscape?

c Use simple diagrams to explain the process of salt harvesting.

6 Re-read the information on managing the Carmargue.

a What is the aim of the French Regional Parks?

b What is being done in the Camargue to help conserve the area?

c Do you think that areas like the Camargue should be conserved? Explain your answer.

Some people feel that the salt industry spoils the natural environment and that the heavy lorries, taking away the salt, pollute the area.

Tourism

Almost one million tourists visit the Camargue each year to see the wildlife and enjoy the many kilometres of wide, open sandy beaches. Whilst tourism has bought money to the area and increased employment, it has also led to problems such as noise and pollution from cars, congestion on the narrow roads, cars parking on roadsides damaging vegetation, and lead shot, used by hunters, being eaten by water-birds and poisoning them.

Managing the Camargue

The need to manage and protect the area was recognised in 1972 when it became a Regional Park – the Parc Naturel Regional de Camargue. The aim of this, and the other parks in France, is to protect the natural character of the area, whilst allowing access to visitors.

Tourism, salt harvesting and farming are allowed to take place in certain zones only and traditional land uses such as grazing have been encouraged. Some areas have been set aside for scientific research. Visitor centres and nature trails have also been established to inform tourists about the need to conserve and protect the wildlife of the area.

Map study: Petit Rhône (1:25 000)

The following activity relates to Figure 4.7, a map extract of part of the Camargue.
Look back to Figure 4.3 to locate the area shown on the map extract.

1 Use the scale to work out the width of the river at X.
- What is the name of the river?

2 Look at the area to the west of the river.

a What is the main agricultural land use?

b Why is there so much of this type of land use?

c Why is there a need for 'temporary water courses'?

3 Look at the area to the east of the river.

a What has been built here to protect the area from flooding?

b Look carefully at the line of the embankment. What in particular is it built to protect?

4 Locate the one small area of 'broussailles' on the map.

a What does 'broussailles' mean?

b What is the name of the building located roughly in the middle of this area?

5 Describe the location of the marshes on the map.

6 Draw a sketch map to show some of the main features on the map extract.

a Draw your sketch map to the same scale as Figure 4.7 (9 cm x 15 cm). Use the grid squares to help you make an accurate copy.

b Use a pencil to draw the following features:
- the river
- a river meander
- the main road (the D38)
- the area of rice fields
- the embankment to the east of the river
- the etangs and marshes
- the area of broussailles
- the direction of river flow (show this with an arrow).

c Complete your sketch map by using colours, adding a key, scale and north point as well as a title.

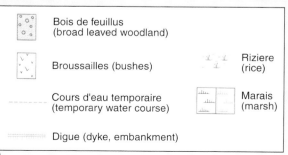

▲ **4.7 Map extract of part of the Camargue, 1:25 000**

Sweden

Sweden is one of the newest members of the European Union, having joined with Austria and Finland in 1995. It is a fascinating country, twice the size of the UK, but with only a tiny population of 8.8 million people. Over half the country is forest and there are some 100 000 lakes. The north is remote, wild and most commonly used for reindeer herding whereas the south, with its capital city Stockholm, is much more urbanised.

1 Getting to know Sweden

▼ 1.1 Some facts about Sweden

Sweden covers an area of 450 000 km². Its area is almost twice that of the UK. Sweden has a similar area to Spain, California and Thailand.

Stockholm is Sweden's capital city. With a population of only 700 000 it is one of Europe's smallest capital cities.

Most of Sweden is low-lying. Its mountains lie along the western border with Norway. The highest mountain is Kebnekaise at 2114 metres. This compares to Mont Blanc in France, the highest mountain in Western Europe, which has a height of 4807 metres.

Most of Sweden's rivers drain from west to east, flowing into the Gulf of Bothnia. Several are used to generate hydro-electric power.

Although only 8 per cent of Sweden is used for farming, the country is 80 per cent self-sufficient in food.

Southern Sweden has cold winters but relatively warm summers. However, northern Sweden becomes extremely cold in the winter and has 24 hours of darkness. On clear nights it is possible to see the 'northern lights'. In the summer, it stays light throughout the night!

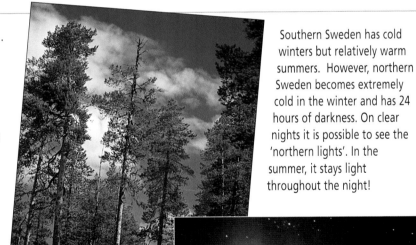

Sweden has a thriving industrial sector. It has a history of shipbuilding and engineering and its well known companies include Saab, Volvo and Scania. Its forests provide wood for paper making and furniture.

Sweden has large deposits of iron ore in the north of the country near Kiruna. It also has other metals such as uranium but little coal or oil. Electricity is generated mainly from water power, imported oil and nuclear power. There are plans to phase out nuclear power by the year 2010.

Throughout the country there are large numbers of elk, deer and fox. There are also bears in the far north.

Sweden is an expensive country to live in but standards of living are very high. It also has one of the highest life expectancy rates in the world.

Like the UK, Sweden has a monarchy. King Carl XVI Gustaf has been the Head of State since 1973.

One of Sweden's traditions is the 'smorgasbord' which is a buffet consisting of a variety of home produced foods, particularly fish.

Sweden has a 'law of common access', which means that people have the right to walk and pick berries in the forests and the fields without asking the landowner's permission. They are in turn expected to treat the countryside with respect.

KEY

Relief
metres

5000
3000
2000
1000
500
200
sea level

Permanent ice

▲4808 Mountain height (in metres)

River
Intermittent river
Canal
Lake / Reservoir
Marsh
International boundary
◼ Capital cities
▫ Other town or city
● Large town or city
○ Other town or city

SCALE 1 : 7 500 000

0   100   200   300 km

© Bartholomew Ltd 1999

North Cape
Magerøya
Hammerfest
Sørøya
Lopphavet Seiland
Porsangen
Laksefjorden
Kongsfjorden
Vadsø
Varangerfjorden
Kirkenes
Zapolyarnyy
Nikel
Murmansk
Kola
Ringvassøy
Kvaløya
Tromsø
Jieśjávri
Inarijärvi
Oz. Ekostrova
Kirovsk
Apatity
Monchegorsk
Ulehkkevarri 1833
Senja
Alta
Taivaskero 807
Muonio
Lokan tekojärvi
Oz. Imandra
Kandalaksha
Kandalakskaya
Vesterålen
Andøya
Langøya
Hinnøya
Harstad
Narvik
Torneträsk
Kebnekaise 2114
Akkajaure
Kiruna
Muonio
Kittilä
Sodankylä
Pello
Miekojärvi
Rovaniemi
Suolijärvi
Kemijärvi
Yli-Kitka
Oz. Puaozero
Loukhi
Lofoten
Værøy
Bodø
Sørøkjåkka 2090
Stora Lulevatten
Gällivare
Jokkmokk
337
Kemi
Kemijärvi
Kuusamo
Muojärvi
Oz. Topozero
Solov
Glomfjord
Snøtinden 1594
Mo i Rana
Okskolten 1915
Norra Storfjället 1792
Hornavan
Storavan
Uddjaure
Sorsele
Arvidsjaur
Boden
Alvsbyn
Luleå
Haparanda
Tornio
Simojärvi
Taivalkoski
Oulu
Kiantajärvi
Reboly
Oz. Leksozero
Medve
Vega
Mosjøen
Brønnøysund
Rossvatnet
Storuman
Marsfjället 1589
Storuman
Limingen
Malgomaj
Vilhelmina
Lycksele
Vindel
Robertsfors
Umeå
Skellefte
Skellefteå
Piteå
Raahe
Kalajoki
Pyhä
Oulainen
Oulujärvi
Kajaani
Hyrynsalmi
Kuhmo
Vikna
Namsos
Steinkjer
Flåsjön
Åsele
Vännäs
Kokkola
Haapajärvi
Lestijärvi
Nurmes
Lieksa
Pielinen
Oz. Leksozero
Frøya
Smøla
Hitra
Verdalsøra
Trondheim
Løkken
Støren
Stjørdalshalsen
Strömsund
Östersund
Vännäs
Örnsköldsvik
Vaasa
Jakobstad
Nykarleby
Kristiansund
Andalsnes
Storskrymten 1985
Sylarna 1761
Järpen
Storsjön
Brunflo
Sollefteå
Härnosand
Lihtia
Seinäjoki
Alavus
Kuopio
Kurikka
Suonenjoki
Joensuu
Outokumpu
Pyhäselkä
Orivesi
Sortavala
Ålesund
Molde
Stranda
Røros
Tynset
Hede
Sveg
Ljungan
Sundsvall
Brämön
Närpes
Kauhajoki
Jyväskylä
Jämsänkoski
Pihtipudas
Mikkeli
Saimaa
Imatra
Lake Lado
Måløy
Florø
Sandane
Galdhøpiggen 2470
Gudbrandsdalen
Otta
Älvdalen
Särna
Ljusdal
Hudiksvall
Iggesund
Bollnäs
Söderhamn
Kankaanpää
Näsijärvi
Ylöjärvi
Tampere
Heinola
Lahti
Lappeenranta
Svetogorsk
Vyborg
Sulå
Høyanger
Sognefjorden
Iggeland
Lillehammer
Rena
Elverum
Mora
Siljan
Rättvik
Falun
Sandviken
Gävle
Pori
Vammala
Valkeakoski
Hämeenlinna
Kuhntjärvi
Kouvola
Hamina
Bergen
Voss
1690
Hardangervidda
Harteigan
Mosvatnet
Hønefoss
Lillestrøm
Kongsvinger
Ludvika
Avesta
Rauma
Uusikaupunki
Forssa
Riihimäki
Järvenpää
Hyvinkää
Kirkkonummi
HELSINKI
Vantaa
Espoo
St Petersburg
Sestroretsk
Kiro
Bømlo
Haugesund
Karmøy
Stavanger
Sandnes
Setesdal
1443
Drammen
Ski
Kongsberg
OSLO
Askim
Horten
Tønsberg
Moss
Sarpsborg
Kristinehamn
Karlskoga
Örebro
Köping
Arboga
Västerås Enköping
Sala
Uppsala
Norrtälje
Yrkū
Turku
Åland
Södra Kvarken
Mariehamn
Kärdla
Hiiumaa
TALLINN
Rakvere
Narva
Chudo
Larvik
Skien
Porsgrunn
Fredrikstad
Halden
Åmål
Kumla
Katrineholm
Nynäshamn
Eskilstuna
Södertälje
STOCKHOLM
Hjälmaren
Haapsalu
Saaremaa
Pärnu
Viljandi
Tartu
ESTONIA
Lake Peipus
Pskov
Arendal
Kristiansand
Lindesnes
Lidköping
Vänern
Vänersborg
Uddevalla
Trollhättan
Lilla Edet
Falköping
Alingsås
Lerum
Skövde
Skara
Mariestad
Motala
Vättern
Linköping
Norrköping
Mjölby
Tranås
Sommen
Västervik
Visby
Gotland
Färö
Oskarshamn
Kuressaare
Valga
Valka
Ostrov
Opochka
FEDERATIO
Skagerrak
Göteborg
Hjørring
Brønderslev
Thisted
Skagen
Frederikshavn
Læsø
Falkenberg
Varberg
Kinna
Borås
Nässjö
Eksjö
Jönköping
Värnamo
377
Ljungby
Åsnen
Växjö
Nybro
Öland
Kalmar
Ventspils
Taisi
Gulf of Riga
Venta
Kuldiga
Liepaja
LATVIA
Jelgava
Daugava
Rezekne
Daugavpils
Velikiye
Opochka
Ålborg
Struer
Skive
Hobro
Randers
Grenå
Ängelholm
Hässleholm Karlshamn
Halmstad
Bolmen
Karlskrona
Tukums
Jelgava
Mazeikiai
Šiauliai
Panevezys
Rokiškis
Vitsyeb
DENMARK
Århus
Viborg
Ringkøbing
Holstebro
Herning
Silkeborg
Vejle
Horsens
Esbjerg
Fredericia
Kolding
Ribe
Haderslev
Åbenrå
Hillerød
Helsingør
Helsingborg
Lund
COPENHAGEN
Malmö
Ystad
Kristianstad
Klaipeda
Kedainiai
Gargždai
Siauliai
LITHUANIA
Kaunas
VILNIUS
BELARUS
Barysaw
Sjælland
Korsør
Køge
Næstved
Møn
Trelleborg
Rønne
Bornholm (Denmark)
Sovetsk
Neris
Kaliningrad RUS. FED.
Chernyakhovsk
Sylt
Flensburg
Schleswig
Nyborg
Odense
Svendborg
Fyn
Langeland
Nakskov
Lolland
Falster
Nykøbing
North Frisian Islands
Husum
Neumünster
Nordstedt
Kiel Canal
Fehmarn
Rügen
Sassnitz
Courland Lagoon
Slupsk
Lebork
Gdynia
Baltiysk
Gdansk
Elblag
Malbork
Koszalin
Kaliningrad
MINSK
Kiel
Lübeck
Rostock
Stralsund
Swinoujscie

Norwegian Sea

N   O   R   W   A   Y

S   W   E   D   E   N

Lappland

FINLAND

Gulf of Bothnia

Baltic Sea

Gulf of Finland

RUSSIAN FEDERATION

Arctic Circle

Atlas Map E ▲

1 For the following questions you will need to study Atlas Map E, opposite.

a With which country does Sweden share its longest border?

b Which country lies to the east of the Gulf of Bothnia?

c By what other name is northern Sweden and northern Finland known?

d Which country is separated from Sweden by the Kattegat?

e What is the name of the sea that separates Sweden from Lithuania and Latvia?

f Vanern is the largest what in Sweden?

g Which is further south, Stockholm or Norway's capital city Oslo?

h Locate the city of Goteborg on Sweden's west coast. Is it to the east or west of the Danish capital city, Copenhagen?

i Which Swedish town lies closest to the Arctic Circle?

j Locate Malmo in the far south of Sweden and Kiruna in the far north. Use a ruler and the scale to work out the distance between the two settlements.

2 Draw a map to show the main features of the geography of Sweden and the surrounding area. On a blank outline of Sweden or a copy of Figure 1.2, locate and label the following features using Atlas Map E, page 110, to help you. (Remember to use a pencil first and then colours and ink.)

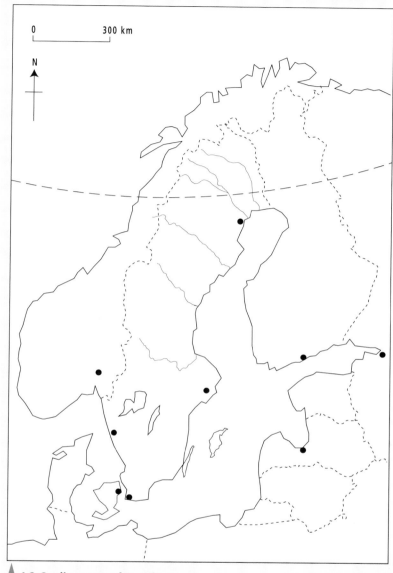

1.2 Outline map of Sweden

Towns/cities ● Stockholm ● Pitea ● Kiruna ● Jokkmokk ● Goteborg ● Malmo ● Oslo ● Copenhagen ● Riga ● St Petersburg ● Helsinki

Lakes ● Vanern ● Vattern

Rivers ● Torne ● Lule ● Vindel ● Indals ● Vasterdal

Mountain ● Kebnekaise (2114 m)

Seas/oceans ● Norwegian Sea ● Baltic Sea ● Gulf of Bothnia ● Skagerrak ● Kattegat ● Gulf of Finland

Islands ● Gotland ● Oland

Countries ● Sweden ● Norway ● Denmark ● Finland ● Latvia ● Russian Federation ● Estonia ● Lithuania ● Poland ● Germany ● area known as Lappland.

3 Look at Table 1.3.

a Calculate the percentage for 'Other land uses'.

b What land uses do you think make up the 'Other land uses'?

c Present the information in the form of a proportional bar. To do this, draw a bar 10 cm high and 2 cm wide. Now divide the bar to show each of the percentage figures using a vertical scale of 1 cm = 10%. Use a colour key for each land use or symbols of your choice.

4 Sweden is well known as an 'outdoors' country.

a Name some outdoor activities that people might participate in, given the huge areas of forest, mountains, lakes and rivers in Sweden.

b What is the 'law of common access'?

c Do you think it is a good idea? Why?

d How do you think such a law would work in the UK? Explain your answer.

5 Table 1.4 compares the climate of Stockholm (southern Sweden) with that of Pitea (northern Sweden). Both places are located on Figure 1.2.

a Draw two climate graphs to compare the two sets of data. Look back to page 14 to remind you how to draw a climate graph. Make sure that your vertical scales are identical so that the two graphs can be compared. Use a blue line to show the minimum temperatures and a red line to show the maximum temperatures.

b Which is the warmest month in both Stockholm and Pitea?

c Compare the winter temperatures for Stockholm and Pitea.

d Why do you think that summers in Pitea are described as being 'surprisingly warm'?

e Which is the wettest season in both Stockholm and Pitea?

f What evidence is there that the precipitation from November through to March is more likely to be in the form of snow rather than rain?

g Which place has the highest average annual precipitation? Include the figures in your answer.

▼ **1.3**

Land use in Sweden	%
Forest	54%
Mountains	16%
Farmland	8%
Lakes and rivers	9%
Other land uses	?
Total	100%

▼ **1.4 Climatic data for Stockholm and Pitea, Sweden**

	J	F	M	A	M	J	J	A	S	O	N	D
Stockholm												
Average daily minimum temp.(C)	-5	-5	-4	1	6	11	14	13	9	5	1	-2
Average daily maximum temp.(C)	-1	-1	3	8	14	19	22	20	15	9	5	2
Average monthly precipitation (mm)	43	30	25	31	34	45	61	76	60	48	53	48
Pitea												
Average daily minimum temp.(C)	-13	-14	-11	-4	2	8	12	10	5	0	-6	-10
Average daily maximum temp.(C)	-6	-6	-1	5	11	17	21	19	13	6	0	-3
Average monthly precipitation (mm)	37	25	23	28	30	47	50	68	69	48	48	44

Source: World Weather Guide, Hutchinson

2 The Sami reindeer herders of northern Sweden

▲ *2.1 The unspoilt landscape of Lappland*

Northern Sweden is a bleak and wild environment with forests, mountains and fast flowing rivers (see Photo 2.1). There are few settlements and no major roads. The climate is very harsh with cold and snowy winters and only a few hours of daylight throughout the winter months.

This part of Sweden is known as **Lappland**. It is the traditional home of a group of people called Lapps or **Sami**.

▲ *2.2 The Sami people have lived in Scandinavia for thousands of years*

Who are the Sami people?

The Sami people (see Photo 2.2), as they prefer to be known, have lived in northern Scandinavia for at least 2 000 years. They used to be **nomadic**, which means that they moved from place to place without having a permanent home. Some were hunter gatherers living off fish and wild animals and berries picked in the forests. Others were involved in reindeer breeding.

1 Study Photo 2.1.

a Write a brief description of the landscape of northern Sweden.

b Does the landscape appeal to you? Explain your answer.

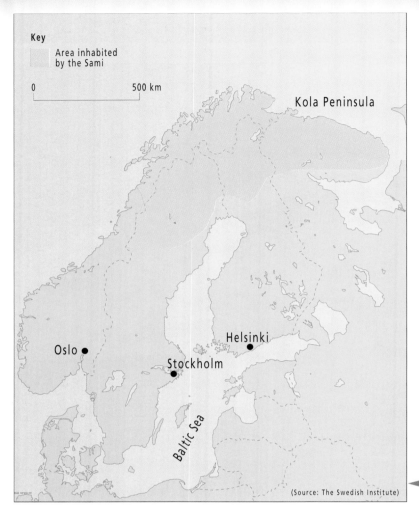

Key

Area inhabited by the Sami

0   500 km

Kola Peninsula

Oslo

Helsinki

Stockholm

Baltic Sea

(Source: The Swedish Institute)

Today there are thought to be about 58 000 Sami people in Sweden, Norway and Finland. Whilst most live in Norway, the largest area occupied by the Sami is in northern Sweden (see Figure 2.3).

In recent years, the Sami people's way of life has been under threat from forestry companies who want to use their grazing lands to plant trees. The Sami people feel that they should have rights to the land that they have used in a traditional way for centuries. They also want to preserve their culture and language. Today Sami interests are represented by an elected agency called the **Sameting** which advises the government on Sami affairs.

2.3 The shaded area on the map is inhabited by the Sami.

2 Look at Figure 2.3.

a Draw a sketch map to show the distribution of the Sami people in Scandinavia. Use Atlas Map E, page 110, to help you locate and label the following:
- Stockholm
- Jokkmokk (the main Sami town in northern Sweden)
- Gulf of Bothnia
- Arctic Circle
- Norway
- Russia.
- Atlantic Ocean
- Sweden
- Finland

b Look at Table 2.4. Present this information in the form of a chart or diagram of your choice. You could draw either:

a **pie chart** (remembering to multiply the percentages by 3.6 to give you the number of degrees) or,

proportional bars onto the sketch map that you drew for the first part of the activity. Place each bar over the appropriate country. Be careful to choose a vertical scale for your bars that fits your map.

c Write a couple of sentences describing the distribution of the Sami people in Scandinavia.

2.4 Distribution of Sami people in Scandinavia

Sweden	17 000 (29%)
Norway	35 000 (60%)
Finland	4 000 (7%)
Kola Peninsula, Russia	2 000 (4%)
TOTAL	58 000 (100%)

Reindeer herding

Reindeer used to roam wild in the forests and mountains of northern Sweden. They became well adapted to the harsh conditions. In the winter they foraged for plants in the forests and, in the summer, they moved to the higher mountain grass pastures. Figure 2.5 describes their seasonal migrations.

Reindeer were first bred to be used as pack animals for transporting goods, rather like horses or donkeys. They were then bred for their meat and for their skins and antlers. Their skins were used to make coats, hats, gloves and bags. Their antlers were carved to make jewellery and household objects such as handles. The reindeer were traded for tools and other items.

In the past the small Sami groups of herders, called Siida, stayed with the reindeer throughout the year. They were nomadic and lived only in temporary shelters. Nowadays they live in permanent settlements such as the town of Jokkmokk (see Atlas Map E, page 110).

About 35 per cent of Sweden's land area is used for reindeer breeding. There are an estimated 300 000 reindeer cared for by about 3 000 Sami. Modern equipment is now used, including two-way radios, snow mobiles, motorcycles and even helicopters!

2.5 Seasonal migration of reindeer

The reindeer herding year

The reindeer are allowed to wander over large areas but they are herded together several times during the year for sorting, marking or slaughter. There is a clear seasonal pattern to the reindeer herding and the Sami have retained the natural reindeer migration patterns as shown in Figure 2.5.

2.6 Reindeer are herded together and marked in the summer ▼

Spring. In the Spring the calves are born.

Summer. The animals are taken to graze the higher summer pastures. It is cooler here and there are fewer mosquitoes to bother the reindeer.The reindeer are gathered together during the summer to be marked (see Photo 2.6).

Autumn. In the Autumn the reindeer are brought together so that some can be slaughtered. It is mainly the males who are slaughtered as the females will provide calves for future years.

Winter. The reindeer are brought down to the forests for the winter and are often split into smaller groups to enable the Sami to keep a more careful eye on them during the long winter months. During the winter the animals survive by scratching through the snow to eat lichens and moss.

3 Read about the Sami reindeer herders.

a Why do the Sami breed reindeer?

b Why do reindeer spend the winters in the forests?

c Why do they move to the higher mountain pastures in the summer?

d How is modern technology used by the Sami in herding reindeer?

e How might the following factors affect the reindeer and the Sami's system of farming?
- trees are cut down for timber and forests are lost
- lichen grows extremely slowly and is harmed by air pollution

4 Make a large copy of Figure 2.5. Using the text, add as many labels as you can to describe and explain the seasonal movement of the reindeer.

5 Draw a diagram to illustrate the reindeer herding year. Look back to the chapter on Farming for some ideas. You could show the information in the form of a circular flow diagram, as this system of farming repeats itself each year.

6 The Sami are a minority group within Sweden yet they have lived in northern Sweden for centuries.

a Although they don't own the land, do you think they still have the right to use it?

b How important is it to preserve the culture (crafts and traditions) and language of minority groups like the Sami?

3 Forests in Sweden

Over half of Sweden is covered by trees. Sweden's relatively cold, sheltered and humid climate favours the growth of the **northern coniferous forests**. The most common type of tree found in the coniferous forests is the Norway spruce (see Photo 3.1). Deciduous trees grow in southern Sweden because the conditions are warmer.

What are the trees used for?

In the past the forests provided wood for building and for fuel. Some wood was processed and turned into charcoal to be used as fuel in Sweden's early industries to smelt metals.

▲ *3.1 Norway spruce trees grow in cold climates*

Look at Figure 3.3. It describes the main uses of the wood from Sweden's forests. Nowadays, most of the timber is used to make paper or products such as chipboard for the building industry. Most of the pulp and paper mills (where the timber is processed) are found at the coast (see the map in Figure 3.3) so that the products can be easily exported. While some of the timber is still floated down the rivers to the coast (see Photo 3.2) most is now transported by lorry.

▲ *3.2 Timber is brought to the paper mills by river*

▼ *3.3 Some uses of wood in Sweden's forests*

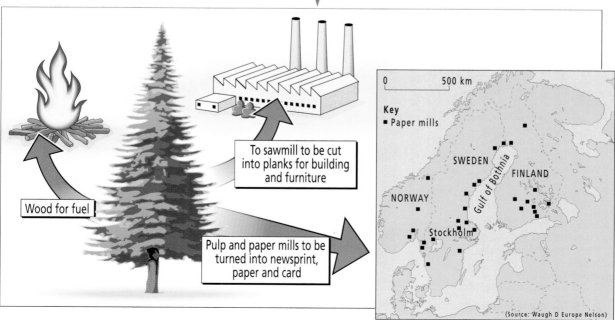

Wood for fuel

To sawmill to be cut into planks for building and furniture

Pulp and paper mills to be turned into newsprint, paper and card

Key
■ Paper mills

SWEDEN

FINLAND

Gulf of Bothnia

NORWAY

Stockholm

0   500 km

(Source: Waugh D Europe Nelson)

1 Read about Sweden's forests.

a How much of Sweden is covered by forest? (See Figure 1.3 page 112).

b Why is northern Sweden well suited to coniferous trees?

c There are two types of tree – coniferous and deciduous. Do you know the differences between them?

2 Make a list of as many items as you can that are made from wood. Use Figure 3.3 to help you get started. Once you have made your list, present your information in the form of a colourful poster, perhaps with a picture of a tree in the centre as in Figure 3.3.

3 Look at Table 3.4 which lists the different wood products that make up Sweden's forest exports. Forest products make up 17% of Sweden's total exports by value.

▼ *3.4*

Product	% of total forest products exported (by value)
paper	50
wood pulp	13
sawn goods	24
other wood products (e.g. for building)	13
Total	100

a Draw a pie chart to show the information in Table 3.4. Use different colours and a key.

b During the last 30 years the demand for paper worldwide has increased dramatically. Why do you think this has happened?

c Nowadays a lot of paper is being recycled. Why do you think this is happening?

d Can you name some everyday items that are made from recycled paper? Have a look at home and around your school.

This series of illustrations describe the management of a typical private forest. Notice that forestry involves a rotation. in this way it is sustainable and will provide future generations with timber. It also preserves natural habitats and wildlife.

Replanting (2)
Aim: To ensure rapid and reliable regrowth for suitable species of trees on the site.
When: As soon as possible after soil preparation.
How: Planting and sowing is mainly done manually.

Thinning (3)
Aim: To harvest part of the forest in order to create high-quality timber and to provide conditions for continued production.
When: One or more thinnings when trees are a few metres tall.
How: Today thinning is usually done mechanically, but sometimes also manually with a power saw.

Final felling (1)
Aim: To harvest the forest and create conditions for regeneration.
When: After 60 – 150 years depending on tree species and location.
How: Mechanical final-felling.

▲ *3.5 The management of a Swedish forest.*

Managing forests

During the nineteenth century some people became concerned about the rate of forest clearance. In 1903 the Forestry Act demanded that forests be managed more **sustainably** so that they would benefit future generations. Trees had to be replanted once areas had been cleared.

Through careful management, the amount of forest in Sweden has actually increased and today about 120 000 people are employed in forest-related jobs.

Look at Figure 3.5. It describes the management of a typical forest in Sweden. Can you see that the separate processes form a kind of cycle? As old trees are cut down, so new trees are planted. In this way, the forest becomes sustainable for future generations.

▲ *3.6 The Seri Nature Reserve*

Why are the forests special?

A forest is much more than just an industrial raw material. It is a special environment with its own unique habitats, plants and animals. Some areas of forest in Sweden are protected as nature reserves.

One such reserve is the Serri Nature Reserve in northern Sweden (see Photo 3.6) It has been carefully managed to allow people to visit the forest and enjoy the trees, plants and animals. Camping is encouraged, barbecue areas have been built and there is fuelwood already chopped in nearby huts. There are also many walks. On some paths boards have been put down to prevent damage to the undergrowth. The Swedes' love of nature is demonstrated by the complete lack of vandalism or litter in these areas.

---

4 Study Figure 3.5.

a Present the information in Figure 3.5 in the form of a circular flow diagram to show how forest management forms a cycle.

b What does the term 'sustainable' mean?

c Why is the system of management shown in Figure 3.5 sustainable?

5 Study Photo 3.6 and read about the Serri Nature Reserve.

a What are the natural attractions of Serri Nature Reserve?

b What has been done to help people enjoy the reserve?

c How do we know that the Swedes love their natural environment?

6 In Sweden everyone has the right of access to the countryside. Design a poster for display in the Serri Nature Reserve informing English-speaking visitors about the rules of the Swedish 'right of access'. Use simple sketches or diagrams to illustrate the points listed here and keep your writing to a minimum. You might like to work in pairs or small groups.

Sweden's 'right of public access'

- do not approach too close to houses
- shut gates after you
- do not pitch tents too close to houses and to other people's tents
- do not light fires on bare rocks because they may crack or split. Use the barbecue pit provided.
- do not leave litter and do not leave bags of litter for animals to open and spread around
- do not cut trees or bushes
- fishing is allowed in the lakes but only with a rod and line

4 Stockholm : European city of culture 1998

Stockholm is one of Europe's most beautiful capital cities. It is built on 14 islands where the freshwater Lake Malaren meets the Baltic Sea (see Figure 4.2). Its many elegant and historic buildings are set among green parks, water and bridges and it is well known for its fresh air and open spaces (see Photo 4.1). From the map in Figure 4.3, you can see that only a third of Stockholm is shops and buildings, another third is parks and woodland and the final third is water. It is easy to see why Stockholm was Europe's **city of culture** in 1998.

The history of Stockholm

Find the area named Gamla Stan (old town) on Figure 4.3. This was the original site of Stockholm.. The first fortification was built here

4.1 A panoramic view of central Stockholm

in 1255 and for several centuries the town remained here before spreading onto neighbouring land. It is easy to imagine that such a **site** was easy to defend.

Up until the middle of the nineteenth century, much of the built-up area of the city would have been very unpleasant. There were open sewers, crowded slums, no piped water and no pavements. Nowadays it is very different. Gamla Stan has many grand buildings and narrow medieval streets and alleys. It is very popular with tourists. With its colourful boats moored along the rivers, its Royal Palace (see Photo 4.4) and museums, and its wealth of cinemas, shops and restaurants, Stockholm is a busy and vibrant European city.

4.2 The city of Stockholm has been built on a collection of islands linked by bridges

E4, Uppsala, Norrtälje, Arlanda (International Airport), E18, Västerås, E18, E4, E18, Laka Målaren, Vaxholm, Möja, E20, Sandhamn, Eskilstuna, STOCKHOLM, E4, Nynäshamn, N, 0 20 km

(Source: Scandinavia Rough Guide Brown J & Sinclair M)

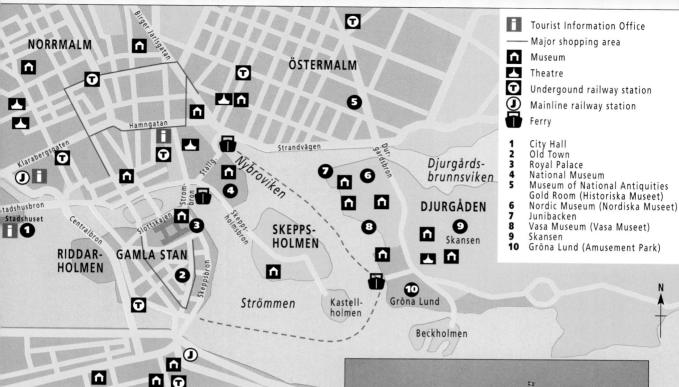

4.3 Street map of Gamla Stan

4.4 The Royal Palace ▶

1 Look at the map in Figure 4.3.

a Where was the original site of Stockholm?

b Why would it have been an easy site to defend?

c Describe how Stockholm was a very different place in the nineteenth century compared to today.

2 The following questions relate to the map of central Stockholm, Figure 4.3.

a Find the City Hall at the point marked 1. Why would the City Hall be a good place for a tourist to visit?

b Apart from the Old Town, what is the main attraction on Gamla Stan?

c There are lots of museums on Figure 4.3. What is the Swedish word for 'museum'?

d Why might you visit the Vasa Museum?

e One of the most popular tourist sites is Skansen, the world's oldest open-air museum. On what island is Skansen?

3 Look at Figure 4.3. You have just visited the Royal Palace on Gamla Stan. You now want to travel to Skansen by ferry. Now look closely at the route and try to answer the following questions:

a Along which street do you walk from the Royal Palace to the ferry terminal?

b What is the name of the area of water that your ferry crosses?

c Which small island do you go round?

d Your ferry arrives at Grona Lund. What could you visit there before walking on to Skansen?

e What else could you visit at Skansen?

f After visiting Skansen you return to the ferry terminal but take a different ferry. Where does it take you?

The Stockholm Archipelago

One of the unique features of Sweden's capital city is the Stockholm archipelago. The word '**archipelago**' means a collection of islands. There are many examples of archipelagos across the world. One of the most famous is the collection of islands in the Aegean Sea (such as Crete and Rhodes) which are part of Greece.

Lying just to the east of the city at the edge of the Baltic Sea are some 24 000 islands which make up the Stockholm archipelago (see Figure 4.5). About 150 islands are large enough to be permanently settled, but most are very small

rocky outcrops covered in pine trees. The archipelago is a holiday paradise for Stockholmers during the summer. Several holiday companies operate ferries and small boats in the area, and thousands of people visit the islands to enjoy the sandy beaches, the wildlife and the peace and quiet.

In the past the islands had a different use. They provided the people of Stockholm with protection from their enemies. Hostile foreign ships were unable to find their way through the islands. It must have been rather like being in a massive maze!

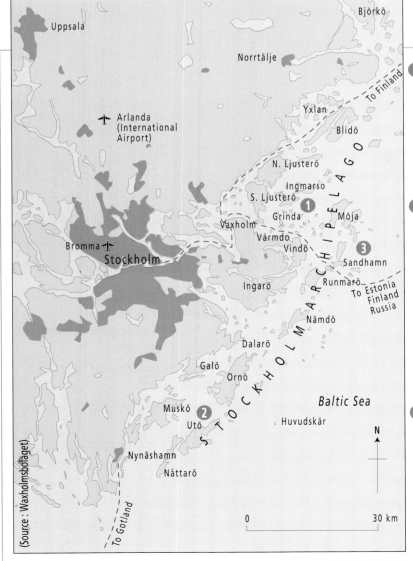

4.5 there is a lot to do on a holiday in the islands of the archipelago

① Grinda
The island of Grinda is two hours from Stockholm. It's a popular spot for Stockholmers to go for a swim or just relax in the meadows and it's only a 15-minute walk from one end of the island to the other.

② Uto
Uto, which is 3 hours from Stockholm, is probably the most complete tourist site in the whole archipelago. There are many facilities including a hotel, a youth hostel, restaurants, swimming and camping sites, bicycle hire, a guest harbour, and a chance to do some fishing. The oldest iron mine in Sweden is on Uto, and there is a small mining museum on the island.

③ Sandhamn
Sandhamn, which is 3 hours from Stockholm, is the main centre for sailing and the Royal Swedish Yacht Club was established here. Near the harbour there are a couple of hotels, restaurants and shopss. With its fine sandy beaches, it is an ideal place for swimming and scuba diving.

4 Look at the map in Figure 4.5.

a What is an 'archipelago'?

b How many islands are there in the Stockholm archipelago?

c Use the photographs in Figure 4.5 to describe what the islands in the archipelago look like.

d How did the islands provide Stockholm with protection from hostile ships in the past?

5 Study the three photos in 4.5.

a Why do you think Stockholmers want to get away from the city in the summer?

b Make a list of the main attractions of the archipelago to the people of Stockholm.

c What holiday activities can you see in the photos?

6 Write a short article advertising the Stockholm archipelago to appear in an English-speaking magazine that is running a feature about visiting Stockholm. Use sketches and other illustrations if you wish but remember that your article is an advert intended to encourage people to visit the islands.

There is further information on the Stockholm archipelago on the Internet. Look up the Stockholm Information Service at "www.stoinfo.se".

Published by Collins Educational
An imprint of HarperCollins*Publishers* Ltd
77-85 Fulham Palace Road
London W6 8JB

The HarperCollins website is:
www.**fire**and**water**.com

© HarperCollins*Publishers* Ltd
First published 1999
Reprinted 2000

ISBN 0 00 326695 8

Project management and editing by Susan Millership
Illustration management by Wendi Watson
Picture research by Charlotte Lippmann
Cover design by Derek Lee
Internal design by Glynis Edwards
Page layouts by Janet McCallum/Wendi Watson
Illustrations by Cedric Knight, John Elsey, Belinda Evans and Paula Knock
Production by Anna Pauletti
Printed and bound by Printing Express Ltd., Hong Kong.

Acknowledgements

Richard Young, Photo Air
The German Information Centre
The National Farmer's Union
Oliver Dowding at Avaries Farm
National Energy Authority in Iceland
EDF (Electricité de France)
Mrs V Aubry, French Embassy, London
Eurotunnel Education Service
Tonga Rescue Service
The Swedish Institute
The Stockholm Information Service
Chris Dolan
Mike Watson Photography

Dedication

To Mum with love

Acknowledgements Photographs
Every effort has been made to contact the holders of
copyright material, but if any have been inadvertently
overlooked the publishers will be pleased to make the
necessary arrangements at the first opportunity.

Aerofilms: 40
Ecoscene : 35mr/Martin Jones, 35bl/Nick Hawkes, 86
EDF 98/Claude Paquet
Eye Ubiquitous: 17ml/Julia Waterlon
FPLA 109br/W Wisniewski
Frank Lane Picture Agency: 17b/L G Nilsson, 105t/M.B.
Withers, 105b/Gerard Lacz, 117ml/W. Wisniewski,
116/B. Geijerstam, 113t/Gosta Hakansson
Greenpeace 61tr
James Davis: 106, 120tr, 121mr
Jon Nash:72
Natural History Photographic Agency: 31br/David
Woodfall
National Farmer's Union 47t
Ordnance Survey © Crown copyright:27bl, 42t
Photoair: 21, 27t, 75
Popperfoto: 32br/Gustau Nacarino/Reuters,
94t/AFP/Rabih Moghrabih
Robert Harding: 56mr/Hans Peter Merten 108br/Michio
Hoshino
Saab: 109tr
Science Photo Library: Cover, 4t, 71
Serie Bleu 107tr
Simon Ross:20t, 22b, 22tr, 23t, 24tr, 25tl, 38t, 41,43t,
69, 70, 76tr, 108ml, 113br, 119tr
Still Pictures: 56t, 64/Thomas Raupach
Stuart Rae: 19tr
Swedish Travel and Tourism Council 122b, 123b
Texaco Ltd: 60
The Image Bank: 13ml/Frans Lemmens, 29t,
55/Anthony Johnson, 96/Hans Wolf, 91/Isy-Schwart,
84ml/Marc Loiseau, 101/Pascal Perret
Tony Stone Images: 32tr/Johnny Johnson, 94m/Jeremy
Walker, 100t/Fernand Ivaldi, 100br/John Higginson,
81/Michael Busselle
Trethorne Leisure Farm: 51
Woodfall Wild Images : 12t, 16b, 18bl, 34b, 43b, 48br,
80, 84b, 85, 87, 88/David Woodfall, 48ml/Mike Powles,
49tr/Andreas Leeman, 62/Val Corbett, 68, 77/Tom
Murphy, 94b/Jeremy Moore, 117tr/Maurizio Biancaelli

abrasion 70
acid rain 66
Alps 68-71, 73, 78-9, 91, 94
aquifers 89
artificial fertilisers 31, 41
atmosphere 12, 80-81
avalanche protection 79
avalanches 68, 77-9
Aviaries Farm 40-47

blending 102

Camargue 91, 103-107
Champagne 100-102
Channel Tunnel 94
chemicals 31-2, 41, 87-90
Chernobyl reactor 97
Cherry Tree Farm 53
chloropleth maps 8-9
cirque 71
climate 12-19
    Arctic climate 15
    continental climate 15-16
    Mediterranean climate 15-18
    mountain climate 15
    northern European climate 17
    sub-Arctic climate 15, 19
    temperate climate 15-16
climate graph 14
coal 30, 95
Common Agricultural Policy (CAP) 54-55
condensation 81
confluence 20-21
continents 4
corries 76
crevasses 69, 71-2
cross-sections 25
crude oil 58-60, 95-6

dams 30, 99
deposition 24
drainage basin 20
dredging 35
drought 18

ecosystems 31
electricity 29-31, 56-7, 62-7, 96
energy 56-67, 95
    non-renewable energy 56-64
    renewable energy 56-64
energy conservation 65-7
environment 54, 56
Environment Agency 36

erosion 22-3, 68, 70, 73-6
etangs 105
European Economic Community (EEC) 4
European Union (EU) 4-7, 9, 54-5
evaporation 81

farm diversification 51
farm systems 38-9
farming 38-55
    cereals 48-50
    dairying 48-50
    Mediterranean farming 48-50
    mixed farming 43-4, 48-50
    organic farming 40-41, 47, 55
    sheep farming 48-50
    reindeer 49-50
fermented 102
flash floods 32-3
flood embankments 35
flood relief channels 35-7
flooding 20, 29, 32-7
floodplain 34
fodder crops 43, 46
food surpluses 54-5
forest management 117-119
forestry 114
fossil fuels 56, 58-60, 95-6
France 91-107
frost shattering 68, 70

Galtur 78
Gamla Stan 120-21
glacial trough 74
glaciers 68-74, 76
global warming 66
gradient 30
Great Langdale 74-6
groundwater flow 81

hydro-electric power (HEP) 30-31, 95

ice 68-79
Ice Age 73-4
ice sheets 73-4
icebergs 73
industry 30
inputs 39, 44
irrigation 85-7

La Rance 98-9
land set-aside 55
Lappland 109, 113
latitude 13
Lowtown 37

maps
  atlas maps 10-11, 83, 93
  OS maps 27, 42
  location maps 4-5, 8-9, 12, 15, 21, 28, 33, 36, 40, 49, 52, 59, 63, 68, 73-4, 78, 82, 85-6, 91, 95, 99, 100, 103-104, 109, 111, 114, 117, 120
meander 20, 24-5
Mer de Glace 68-71
milk quota 55
Mistral wind 62
Mont Blanc 68
moraine 70-71
mountains 8, 20, 68-79
mouth (river) 20-21
multinationals 59

National Farmers Union 47
natural gas 59, 95
North Sea 29, 59-60
nuclear power 56-7, 96-7

outputs 39, 44

paper mills 117
Pitea 109-110
place 4-11
plain 84
point bar 24
pollution 31-2, 87-90
power stations 56-58, 97-8
precipitation 14, 19, 81
prevailing winds 16
processes 39, 44
Pyrenees 32, 94

radioactive waste 97
rainfall 16, 18, 34, 80-81, 84-7
reindeer 115-16
Rhine Action Programme 32
Rhone Delta 103-4, 107
right of public access 119
river bank 24, 34
river channel 20, 24, 30, 34-5
river cliff 24
River Coquet 20-27
River Eden
River Rhine 28-32
rivers 8, 20-37
Royal Palace (Stockholm) 121

Sami people 113-16
Seri Nature Reserve 119

silage 43
skiing 72, 77-8
snout (glacier) 71
solar power 56-7, 95
source (river) 20-21, 29
Spain 82-7
steel-making 30
Stickle Tarn 76
Stockholm 108-112, 114, 120-21
Sweden 108-121

tarns 76
temperature 12-16, 19
  average temperature 14
  maximum temperature 14
  minimum temperature 14
thermal power 56-7
tidal power 56-7
tidal range 98
tourism 51-3, 86
trade 5
transpiration 81
transport 20, 29-30
trash screens 89
Treaty of Rome 4
Trethorne Leisure Farm 51-2
tributary 20-21, 24
U-shaped valley 74

undercutting 24

V-shaped valley 22
valley 20-22, 29, 68-70, 73-6, 101
vineyards 29, 100-101
viticulture 100

water 80-90, 85-7
water conservation 86
water cycle 80-81
water pollution 87-90
water supply 82-6
water transfer schemes 86-7
water treatment plants 32
waterfall 23
weather 12-19
web addresses 37, 47, 64, 79
wetlands 54, 103
wind 13, 62-4
wind farms 62-4
wind power 56-7, 62-4
wind speed 52